A COMPREHENSIVE STUDY OF METEOROLOGY AND CLIMATOLOGY

FRANK PHILEMON

A COMPREHENSIVE STUDY OF METEOROLOGY AND CLIMATOLOGY

WRITEN BY: Frank Philemon
P.O.Box, 116,
Liwale-Lindi,
TANZANIA.
+255762426746
naxfra@gmail.com

Printed East Africa by:
NAXFRA MIXED EDUCATION ENRICHMENT.
Liwale District,
Lindi- Tanzania.
Email: naxfra@gmail.com
Mobile: +255 762426746/+255683114202

TABLE OF CONTENTS

ACKNOWLEGMENT

This book is a result of direct and indirect effort and contribution of many people in which I sincerely do admit their effort in the motivating passionate and persistence by contributing the work of this book. I thank a lot the members of academic staff especially the department of geography in all schools I taught for their challenging ideas that developed this book.

I also extend my gratitude to the Heavenly almighty God for His protection and blessings to my life. Other special thanks I extend to my lovely wife Mariam Lucas and students at Liwale high school as well as Naxfra Mixed Education Enrichment for extending their hearts and hands in helping to accomplishing the work of this book.

Vipawa Media and Amazon Company are the last but the least. Thank you for sacrificing your comfort and rights the greater good. God bless you all the individuals who have in their personal and official capacity, contributed in one way or another for realization of this book are sincerely acknowledged; without your effort this book would not have seen the light of day.

Frank Philemon
+255762426746.
naxfra@gmail.com
   © 2019

PREFACE

A **Comprehensive Study of Meteorology and Climatology** is the book that developed through maximization of simplification of basic concepts about aspects of weather and climate. This makes its content easily accessible to all geographers (meteorologists, climatologists) and students in secondary schools, high schools, colleges and universities.

This book has been written with the strong aim of helping geographers and alike in getting in-depth understanding and improving their knowledge and skills in all issues of weather and climate. The author is confident that this book will be an invaluable asset for schools, colleges and universities and that students as well as teachers and lecturers will find it useful in making the teaching and learning process easier, pleasant and more fruitful.

Any efforts and contribution in one way or another incurred by all people so as to accomplish the work of this book is acknowledged; without their support this book would not have been written and seen by all of the people of the universe. I acknowledge all writers that I used their books as references to write the work of this book.

Frank Philemon
+255762426746.
naxfra@gmail.com
© 2019

DEDICATION

This book in a special way, I dedicate to the 5th President of The United Republic of Tanzania (URT), **Dr. John Pombe Joseph Magufuli** in his excellency. His slogan **"Hapa Kazi Tu"** from Swahili language meaning **"Here is Only Hard Working"** had fostered me in accomplishing the work of this book, which I worked on for almost six years in writing and organizing the manuscript. May God bless the President and may God bless Tanzania and her people.

The Fifth President of Tanzania, Dr. John Pombe Joseph Magufuli

7

CHAPTER ONE

GENERAL CONCEPT

The atmosphere is a complex medium, and its mechanism and process are sometimes very complicated. Its nature however is generally expressed in terms of only a few variables, which are measurable. The data thus recorded provides the raw materials for understanding both temporary (weather) and long term (climate) atmospheric conditions.

The variables can be through of as the elements of weather and climate. The most important are: temperature content, pressure and wind. These are the basic ingredients of weather and climate. Measuring how they vary in time and space makes it possible to decipher at least partly the complexities of weather dynamics and climatic patterns. Variation in the climatic elements is frequent, if not continuous over Earth. Such variations are caused by, or at least strongly influenced by certain semi permanent attributes of our planet, which are often referred to as **controls.**

Weather is the atmospheric condition of a place which occurs at a particular short period of time. Weather change from day to day, time to time, and differ place to place. Weather has elements that can be recorded and measure. Cloud cover, atmospheric pressure, humidity, precipitation, sunshine wind and temperature are among of the elements of weather. **Climatology** is the study of physical atmospheric condition particularly weather and climate together with their associated influence on the physical earth.

Meteorology is the scientific study dealing with the atmosphere and its phenomena, including weather and climate. Or, meteorology is the study of the earth's atmosphere, especially of weather forming processes and weather forecasting. Meteorologists focus on forecasting weather. They look at a few basic atmospheric interactions and hope to predict the weather in the next few days. Climatologists take a much larger view of the whole climate or weather idea. They look at how climates are created and what they do to the environment. It is a long-term study of the geographic world.

Functions (Importance) of Meteorology

1. Data collected from meteorological studies helps in determining climatic conditions prevailing at a given place of geographical areas.

2. Calculations and convections of weather forecasting help in constructing synoptic charts that indicates the nature of the atmospheric conditions in different stations.

3. The knowledge of weather conditions helps in taking precautions in order to avoid damage that can be caused by an impending bad weather conditions.

4. It is important in understanding the causes of atmospheric instability and stability in relation to the consequences on the earth's surface.

5. It is used in forecasting of the future trend of the weather, which is very important in present age aviation.

What Makes a Climate?

There are several **factors** go into making a climate which are the same as of those from weather. Those factors also affect what the climate will do. Scientists can then make observations and predictions of what will happen in certain climates. If it is hot today and a storm is coming in, you can guess it will get cooler. More specifically, if it is summer where you live, hot and humid, you might be able to guess that you will have thunderstorms in the evening. These factors usually happen in the atmosphere in the area you are looking at.

There is more water vapor in the air if it is humid. If there is a lot of wind, something is making that wind speed up. It could be a series of mountains, or you could be near the ocean. These factors, they all affect each other. For example, higher temperatures might increase evaporation of water that would then increase humidity.

Temperature: The temperature changes throughout the day. At mid-day the temperature gets hot, the land heats up, and air rises. In a coastal area when the air rises, it is replaced by cool air from the ocean. This creates a breeze. When evening comes, the ground cools and the air over the ocean is warmer. The breeze shifts to move towards the ocean.

Pressure: Atmospheric pressure is another important factor. There are large masses of high and low pressure across the Earth. There are also small changes in air pressure that affect locally. In the borders between high and

9

low pressures you will find storm fronts or smaller changes in weather: temperature, humidity, or cloud cover.

Cloud Cover: The number of clouds and the amount of dust and smog affect local climates by changing the temperature. Increased cloud cover decreases the amount of **energy** hitting the Earth from the Sun. This decrease in energy lowers temperatures. In an extreme example, something called nuclear winter covers the entire planet with clouds. With no sunlight getting through, the plants begin to die.

Humidity: Humidity is a measure of the **water vapor** in the surrounding air. As humidity increases, the chances of rain also increase. The air can only hold so much water vapor before a rain formation. Thunderclouds can be created and violent storms can dump huge amounts of water on the land.

Winds: Wind speed is the factor we will cover. The temperature led to the **on-shore and off-shore winds**. Sometimes these can be nice slow breezes and other times very fast and destructive. We may also encounter situations near the base of mountains where changes in temperature create winds that reach 80 miles per hour.

Changing Climates

Climates may undergo large permanent changes and short-term changes. If you use the rainforest as an example, look at the annual temperatures. They vary in a specific way. If you cut down all of the trees in the forest, the temperatures will heat up. Since it is unlikely the forest will be able to grow back for hundreds of years, you would see a long-term climate change.

Short-term climate changes occur also, as seen with an example like El Niño. El Niño occur every few years and increases winter rainfall on the west coast of North America and slightly to the countries along the Indian Ocean. This phenomenon is not a specific part of the climate type; it is a localized variation in the climate.

Different Scales in temperature

Since we shall discuss about heat, **temperatures**, and energy, let us see about how temperature is measured. The big three scales are **Fahrenheit, Celsius** and **Kelvin**. Even though scientists may use only a few scales to measure temperature, there are dozens of types of devices that measure temperatures. All of these devices are called **thermometers** because they measure temperature. There are thermometers to measure human body temperature, the temperature oven that we use, and even the temperature of liquid, oxygen.

Fahrenheit Scale: Fahrenheit is the classic English system of measuring temperatures. Water freezes at 32 degrees Fahrenheit and boils at 212 degrees Fahrenheit. The scale was created by **Gabriel Daniel Fahrenheit** in **1724** and divides the difference between the boiling point and freezing point of water into **180** equal degrees. If you are probably be asked to convert temperatures back and forth from **Fahrenheit** to **Celsius**. Here is the formula: **(Fahrenheit-32)*5/9 = Celsius.**

Celsius Scale: Celsius is the modern system of measuring temperature. It fits in with much of the metric system and has nice round numbers. Water freezes at 0 degrees Celsius and boils at 100 degrees. The scale used to be known as **centigrade** but the name was changed several years ago. Both Celsius and Fahrenheit are used when discussing our day-to-day weather temperatures.

Kelvin Scale: Kelvin scale is an important scale used in most of science. The big thing to remember is that, this is a scale with no units. It offers more than just giving degree amounts. The scale begins at 0 (absolute zero) and just goes up from there. Water freezes at the value 273.15 and boils at 373.15 Kelvin. The word "Kelvin" comes from the person called **Lord Kelvin** who did a lot of work with temperatures.

Note: Temperature scales and measurements also involve *Reaumur* (^{0}R) as a scale of measurement in temperature. 100^0C is equal to 212^0F as equal to 8^0R, while 0^0C = 32^0F = 0^0R. Reading temperatures from thermometer of temperature scales include the followings:

1. Daily or diurnal range of temperature
2. Mean daily temperature
3. Mean monthly temperature
4. Monthly range of temperature
5. Mean annual temperature

CHAPTER TWO

WEATHER AND CLIMATE

By definition **Weather** is the short-term atmospheric conditions for given time and a specific area. Also weather can be defined as the state of physical atmospheric conditions in a given area and usually observed and recorded in short time scales of minutes, two months.

The physical conditions and processes are constantly taking place in the atmosphere and they are subjected to periodic changes over time. The atmosphere reacts by producing an infinitive variety of conditions and phenomena known as collectively as weather. It is the sum of temperature, humidity, cloudiness, precipitation, pressure, winds, storms and other atmospheric variables for a short period of time.

Weather is an almost constant state of change, sometimes in seemingly erratic fashion. Weather notified in hour to hour a day to day. Therefore, the study of atmosphere in which the elements of weather are obtained referred to as **meteorology.** A person who studies weather conditions is known as **meteorologist.** The blanked of gases that envelope the earth and held to the earth by gravity is known as atmosphere (Gravitation force of the earth).

Climate is the average of weather conditions of an area which are observed, recorded and analyzed over a considerable long period of time (usually 30 years or over)

Climate Variety

There are many types of climates across the Earth. You live in one of them or on the border between two. Every year as the **seasons** change, your climate changes a bit. It might get warmer or colder. You might have more or less rain. You might have more or less sunlight that changes all of that other stuff. These are only a few examples:

- Continental: *Hot Summer*
- Continental: *Warm Summer*
- Continental: *Boreal*
- Continental: *Subarctic*

12

- Subtropical: *Dry Summer/Mediterranean*
- Subtropical: *Dry Winter*
- Subtropical: *Humid*
- Subtropical: *Marine West Coast*
- Subtropical: *Wet*
- Tropical: *Monsoon*
- Tropical: *Savannah/Grasslands*
- Tropical: *Wet*
- Polar: *Ice Caps*
- Polar: *Tundra*
- Mountain: *Highlands*

Similarities in Elements of Climate and Weather

The elements of climate are the same as that of weather due to the following reasons:

1) Weather takes into consideration of the changes in these elements at local level and within short time.
2) Climate takes into consideration of these elements in their average over large period of time and at a large scale.
3) The factors that affect weather also influence the climate.

Major Elements and Controls of Weather and Climate

The table below shows about major elements and controls of weather and climate. These also are known as factors that influence climate of a particular place.

ELEMENTS	CONTROLS
Temperature	Latitude and altitude
Pressure	Distribution of land and water
Wind	General circulation of the atmosphere
Moisture content	General circulation of ocean, elevation, topographic barrier and storms

Table2.1: Showing major elements and controls of weather and climate

(a) Latitude and altitude

The continuously changing positional relationship between the sun and Earth brings continuously changing amounts of sunlight, and therefore of radiant energy to different parts of Earth's surface. Thus basic distribution of heat over Earth is first of all a function of latitude. In terms of elements and controls, the control latitude influences the elements temperature.

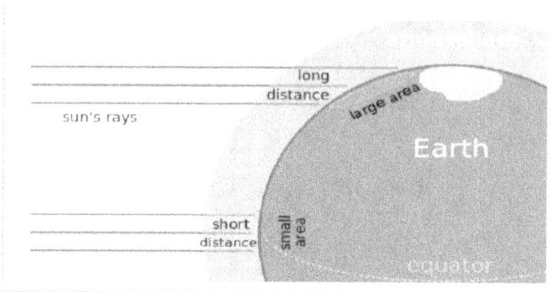

Fig. 2.1: sun rays along latitudes

(b) Distribution of Land and Water

The fundamental distinction concerning the geography of climate is that between continental climates and Martine (oceanic) climates. Oceans heat and cool more slowly and to lesser degree than do landmasses, which means that maritime areas experience milder temperatures than do continental areas in both summer and winter. Also oceans are more abundant source of atmospheric moisture. Thus maritime climates are normally more humid than continental climates. The uneven distribution of continents and oceans over the world is a prominent control of the elements moisture content and temperature.

(c) General Circulation of the Atmosphere.

The atmosphere is in constant motion, with flows that range from transitory local breezes to vast regional wind regimes. At the planetary scale a semi permanent pattern of major wind and pressure systems dominated the troposphere and greatly influences most elements of weather and climate. As a simple example, most surface winds in the tropics come from the east whereas the middle latitudes are characterized by flows that are mostly from the west.

(d) General circulation of oceans.

Somewhat analogous to atmospheric movement are the motions of the oceans. Like the atmosphere, the oceans have many minor motions but also a broad general patterns of currents. These currents assist in heat transfer by moving warm water pole wards and cool water equator wards. Warm currents are found off the eastern coast of contents, and cool currents occur off western coast, a distinction that has a profound effect on coastal climates, **i.e.** Warm currents – warm climate and Cool currents - dry climate.

(e) Elevation.
The three of weather elements – temperature, pressure and moisture contents generally decrease upwards in the atmosphere and are therefore under the influence of the control in the high altitude for example at the top of Kilimanjaro. The water boils there at a low temperature (not 100°C) at these altitudes, so the soup is never really hot.

(f) Topographic barriers.
Mountains and large hills sometimes have prominent effects on one or more elements of climate by blocking or diverting wind flow. The side of a mountain range facing the wind (the windward) side, for example, is likely to have a climate vastly different from that of the sheltered (leeward) side.

Fig. 2.2: leeward and windward of the mountain

(g) Storms.
Various kinds of storms occur over the world. Some have very widespread distribution, whereas others are localized (for example over British Isles). Although they often results from interactions among other climate controls, all storms create specialized weather circumstances and so are themselves considered to be a control. Indeed some storms are prominent and frequent enough to affect not only weather but climate as well. *NB: Others are latitudinal location, vegetation cover, and nature of the soils.*

Influence of climate on human life:
1. Climate influence the style of house construction in a particular area. In the area having strong and heavy rainfall houses have steep roofs while in the areas experiencing low rainfall like in arid areas houses have flat roofs.

2. Conducive climate influence agriculture, transport, settlement, communication among others unlike to the areas having harsh climatic condition.

3. Climate influence dressing styles as in cold regions people worn heavy and wool clothes and in warm region people tend to wear light clothes.

4. Climate influence power generation depending to the nature of an area. The area having water bodies with waterfalls influence hydrological power generation, and areas with abundant wind blow influence for wind power generation.

Elements of Weather

Elements of weather are the basic atmospheric conditions of a place at a given time. The following are the elements of weather:

1. Temperature: Temperature is the degree of hotness or coldness of an object or place. Temperature of an area is measured by using thermometer. Reading of temperature is commonly expressed in a degree of Centigrade or Fahrenheit. The common thermometer which used to measure temperature that measures in term of both maximum and minimum is measured by thermometer called maximum and minimum thermometer.

Temperature readings are normally taken every day at fixed interval or once at 24 hours. Sometimes the self-recording instrument which is known as *thermograph* can record it. Thermograph is found in metrological stations. The higher temperature, the great amount of moisture and vice versa between high temperature results into low atmospheric pressure and vice versa. **Therefore**, temperature of a place can be affected by altitudes, ocean currents, winds, and distance from the sea, vegetation cover, water bodies and human activities.

2. Humidity: Humidity is the amount of water vapor or moisture in the atmosphere. **Moisture** in the atmosphere is formed when the sun heats water bodies like Lake, ocean, rivers, and seas as well as transpiration (by plants). Humidity is measured by Hygrometer that consist wet and dry bulb thermometer.

3. Sunshine: Sunshine refers to the sun's rays that reach the surface of the earth. Sunshine cannot reach on the earth's surface if there are cloud covers in the atmosphere. The intensity of the sunshine is determined by the degree of cloud cover in the sky. Sunshine affects other elements of weather like temperature, humidity etc. Sunshine enables plants to manufacture food through the process of photosynthesis.

4. **Cloud Cover:** Clouds are mixture of water droplets and ice produced by condensation in the atmosphere. Clouds are formed when water vapor cools below ***dew point***. Condensation is the process where water vapor changes into liquid state. Dew point is the temperature at which the atmosphere being cooled and become saturated with moisture.

5. **Wind:** Wind is the movement of air from high pressure to lower pressure. In geography there are two aspects of wind that are important: *(a) Wind direction **and** (b) Wind speed* or *velocity.*

Movement of wind is resulted from thermal differences, which produces pressure variation. Wind is the medium transfer of heat and moisture hence has effects to moisture and heat. The determination of wind direction in its blowing is in two forms: *(a) Sea breeze (occurs day time) and (b) Land breeze (occurs night time)*

6. **Precipitation:** Precipitation is a falling down of water, moisture or frozen water from the atmosphere towards the earth's surface. Also precipitation is defined as the fall or deposition of moisture, water vapor or frozen water from the atmosphere into the earth surface. All life on the earth is partly depending on moisture provided through Precipitation.

7. **Atmospheric pressure:** Atmospheric pressure is the force applied at a point in the earth's surface due to the weight of air above that point. High pressure area called *anticyclones* while the low pressure area is called *cyclones.*

Weather Station

Weather station is the place that set for the purpose of observing, measuring and recording weather elements. Weather stations are found on a meteorological centre, agricultural centre, schools, colleges or universities and government institutions. The following are examples of the common instruments that are found in the weather station for measuring the elements of weather:

(1) A *Thermometer:* measures the air temperature. Most of thermometers are closed glass tubes containing liquids such as alcohol or mercury. When air around the tube heats the liquid, the liquid expands and

moves up the tube, and then the scale shows what the actual temperature is. *Maximum and minimum thermometer (If combined, is called six's thermometer):* Measure temperature of the air.

Maximum thermometer uses mercury to measure the highest temperature reached in a day, while Minimum thermometer have alcohol that used to measure and records the lowest temperature reached a day. Temperature recorded can helps to calculate the total temperature, mean temperature and range of temperature.

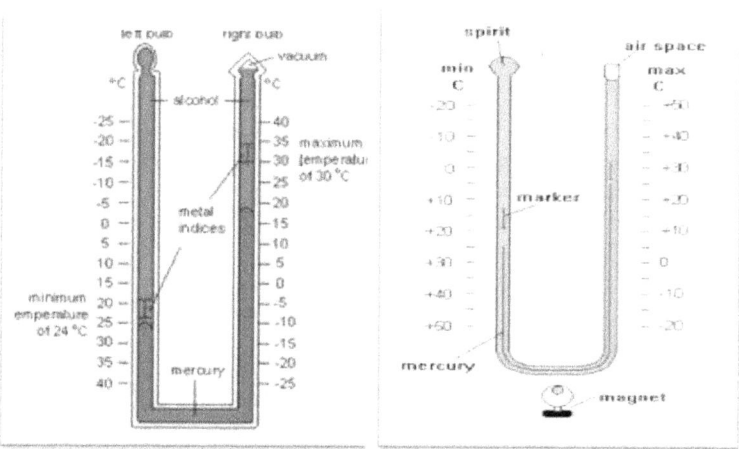

Fig. 2.3 & 2.4: maximum and minimum thermometer

(2) *Hygrometer:* Measure the water vapor content of air or the relative humidity of the air. Hygrometer is into two types: Dry bulb thermometer and Wet bulb thermometer.

Fig. 2.5: Hygrometer

18

(3) *Rain gauge:* Measure the amount of rain that has fallen over a specific time period. Rain gauge collects rain water falling over in a closed vessel. The gauge is placed in an open space far from tree or buildings or other objects. From the obtained data in the rain gauge the following can be determined: *The total rainfall, The range of rainfall* and *The mean rainfall*

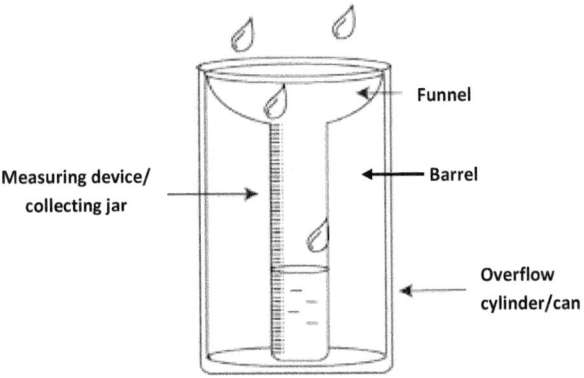

Fig. 2.6: Rain gauge

(4) *Wind vane:* Measure direction of wind blow. Or is an instrument that determines the direction from which the wind is blowing. The velocity of wind is measured by an instrument called *Anemometer.*

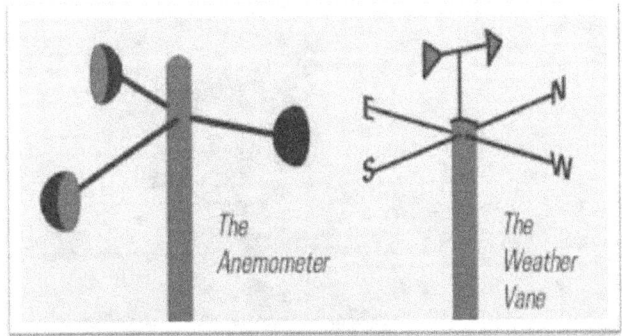

Fig. 2.7: The wind vane and Anemometer

19

(5) *Evaporimeter:* Measure the rate and amount of evaporation. There are two types of evaporimeter: *Piche evaporimeter* measure evaporation from a continuously wet and porous surface. *Tank evaporimeter* it is the pan that contains some level of water. The level of water is measured using Micrometer screw gauge.

(6) *Barometer:* Measures air pressure. It tells us whether or not the pressure is rising or falling. A rising barometer means sunny and dry conditions, while a falling barometer means stormy and wet conditions. An Italian scientist named Torricelli built the first barometer in 1643. There are two types of Barometer: Mercury Barometer and Aneroid Barometer

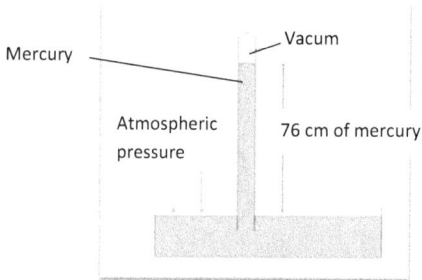

Mercury — Vacum

Atmospheric pressure — 76 cm of mercury

Fig. 2.8: Barometer

(7) *Campbell stoke sunshine recorder:* Measure and record the duration of sunshine

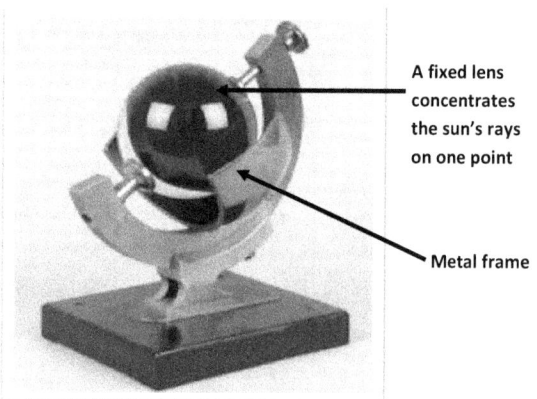

A fixed lens concentrates the sun's rays on one point

Metal frame

Fig. 2.9: Campbell stoke sunshine recorder

How to Establish a Weather Station?

The following are factors to consider for establishing a weather station:

    (1) The place should be an open space of buildings

    (2) The place should be free flow of air

    (3) There should be a wide view for both landscape and sky

    (4) There should be a fence.

    (5) There should be marked by following compass direction

    (6) The ground should be fairly level or gentle slope (not flat) so as the area to be free from floods.

Stevenson's Screen

Stevenson's screen is the white wooden box which is mounted on four legs. It used to house the hygrometer and the thermometer for measuring humidity and temperature. Stevenson's screen is painted by white color both inside and outside so as to reflect sunshine and heat. Stevenson's screen should be above at least 1.2m from the ground in order to avoid heat effects and allow free air movement. The four legs are made of metal to reduce the possibilities of rodents or termites destroying them if they were made of wood.

Fig. 2.10: Open and closed Stevenson's screen

Purposes of Stevenson's screen are:
(1) To provide the conditions necessary for accurate temperature readings.
(2) To ensure the safety of the delicate instruments, such as hygrometer and thermometer.
(3) To protect instruments against precipitation and direct heat outside source.

Weather Forecasting

Weather forecasting is the prediction of weather condition of an area at a given time. In other way, weather forecasting is the application of science and technology to predict the state of the atmosphere for a given location. There are two main methods or ways of weather forecasting as namely below:

1. Traditional weather forecasting

This method is done through observation of natural events occurring within the environment. Normally, this done by aged and experienced persons in the society. Things used in observation are rainbow, crocking of frogs, migration of birds, birds' voices, changing of the wind direction and position of the moon.

2. Modern weather forecasting

This is another method of weather forecasting which involves the use of scientific methods and scientific equipment that used for weather forecasting. This method done by the use of electronic computers, balloons, ships, rockets and records obtained from weather stations. The following are some of the modern weather prediction:

(i) *The radio sound:* Is the instrument used to register pressure and temperature from the ground. The instrument is fixed to the balloons into the atmosphere filled with helium gas. The radio sound on the ground station where they are analyzed. These balloons are made in such a way that they bursts when they reach a certain altitude.

(ii) *Satellites:* Are large electronic devices which sent into space. They move around the earth so as to provide various types of information. They are also used in radio, television and telephone communication.

(iii) *Persistence method:* This is the simplest way of making a weather forecast. Assume that there is no change of the atmospheric conditions.

22

(iv) *Statistical forecasting:* In this method, meteorologists ask themselves. Meteorologists collect records of average temperature and rainfall over the last few years.

Importance of weather forecasting

In forecasting weather, there are number of important of weather forecasting as namely:

1. It enables people to select suitable clothes that depend on the weather condition.

2. It is very important to the airport station that informs the pilots about the weather in the atmosphere, hence to avoid occurrence of accidents.

3. Weather forecasting enables people to be aware with the bad or destructive weather. E.g. Strong wind and drought.

4. Helps farmers to plan better their farms and plantation in their agricultural activities.

5. Weather forecasting is very important to the tourism industry. Tourists may know the weather at the place they expect to go (for leisure, pleasure or study).

6. Very useful in military operations, hence good military operation can be selected.

Names used on maps to indicate lines joining the same area or height of weather elements:

Element Of Weather	Names of the Lines Drawn On The Map
(1) Temperature	Isotherm
(2) Pressure	Isobars
(3) Sunshine	Isohels
(4) Rain fall	Isohyets
(5) Water depth	Isobaths
(6) Height of land above known level	Contours

Table 2.2: Elements of weather and names of lines drawn on the map

23

Elements of Climate and Their Effects

Elements of climate are the factors influencing or affecting climate positively or negatively. Therefore, the following are the effects of the elements of climate:

1. Temperature

Temperature is the degree of hotness or sensible heat. The temperature of the atmosphere is measured by the instrument known as thermometer. The temperature of the atmosphere and the earth's surface is the product of radiation of heat energy received from the sun in the form of *insolation*. Some other founds (minor) includes: Volcanoes, hot springs, human activities which add into atmosphere the greenhouse gases.

Temperature of the atmosphere affects the climate of an area in the sense that:
- ☑ Where the temperature is Low, the climate is cold
- ☑ Where temperature alternate, the climate will have the period of warm and cold season.
- ☑ Where temperature is high, the climate is said to be warm or hot.

2. Precipitation

Precipitation is the general term which refers to the deposition of moisture from the atmosphere on the earth's surface. The rain form of precipitation includes rainfall, snow, mist, forge, dew etc. Other forms precipitation is the result of condition of water vapour formed through evaporation of water from the ground water bodies and plants through evaporation and transpiration respectively (evapotransipiration).

For the precipitation to take place, the following conditions must be fulfilled:
- a) Air must be saturated
- b) Air must have small particles such as dusts on which droplets form.
- c) Air must be cooled to or below dew point.

Therefore, the all forms of precipitation tend to affect the climatic condition at a particular region or place in the sense that:
- a) Where precipitation is heavy, the climate becomes wet.
- b) Where precipitation is low (light), the climate will be dry.
- c) Where precipitation is alternating, the climate will be wet in some periods and dry in others.

3. Atmospheric pressure.

Atmospheric pressure refers to the weight of air exerted by the overhead atmosphere on the unit area of surface. Atmospheric pressure is sometimes known as *Barometric pressure* and it is measured by an instrument known as *Barometer*.

At Sea level, the barometric pressure is about 101^3 mls and decreases with the increases with increases altitude. In statistical, maps atmospheric pressure is shown by using lines called **Isobar.** Isobars are lines drown on the face of maps to join at places with the same barometric pressure. Wind and atmospheric pressure are highly related and they all together affect the climate of an area on the same way. Example: When winds are moving from dry areas they blow they tend to cause drought on that area the reverse is true. When winds are moving from hot areas they tend to rise the temperature of the areas they blow to the reverse also is true.

4. Wind.

Wind is the body of air in motion moving from high pressure area to low pressure area. Wind and atmospheric pressure are highly related and they all together affect the climate of an area on the same way. Example: When winds are moving from dry areas they blow, they tend to cause drought on that area the reverse is true. When winds are moving from hot areas they tend to rise the temperature of the areas they blow to the reverse also is true.

5. Humidity.

Humidity is the amount of water vapour in air. As the air gets warmer, its capacity to hold water vapour increases. This is because as air is heated its molecules move further apart to given room for water vapour to occupy the spaces. When it is cold, molecules move together hence less room for water vapour. Humidity is measured by the wet and dry bulb thermometer known as *Hygrometer* or *Psychrometer*.

6. Clouds cover.

Clouds are the separate masses of visible water vapour floating above the earth's surface (in the lower part of the atmosphere, Troposphere). Clouds are formed when air containing water vapour condenses to form droplets and or ice crystal. Clouds affect the climate of an area in the sense that:

✓ Thick or heavy clouds absorb the incoming solar energy in day time.
✓ They also reflect some of the solar energy in the day.

25

✓ During the night are blankets of the outgoing solar energy.

7. Altitudes.

Altitudes are the height of the ground measured from the mean sea level upwards. Altitudes affect the climate of an area because it influences the temperature. As one goes up in the atmosphere (Troposphere) the temperature decreases at an approximate rate of 0.6°C per 100m or 6°C per 1000m. The rate at which the temperature decreases with the increases in altitude known as *lapse rate* and this is common in the Troposphere.

8. Aspect.

Aspect refers to the direction to which a slope of the land masses faces the sun. The influences of aspect on temperature is more significant in the mid at high latitudes than in the tropics where the sun is always overhead. In the northern hemisphere the South facing slopes receive more **insolation,** thus they are warmer than the south facing slopes.

East vs. West: Northern Hemisphere

Air temps are warmer when afternoon sun shines.

Warmer

Colder

Air temps are colder when morning sun shines.

WEST

EAST

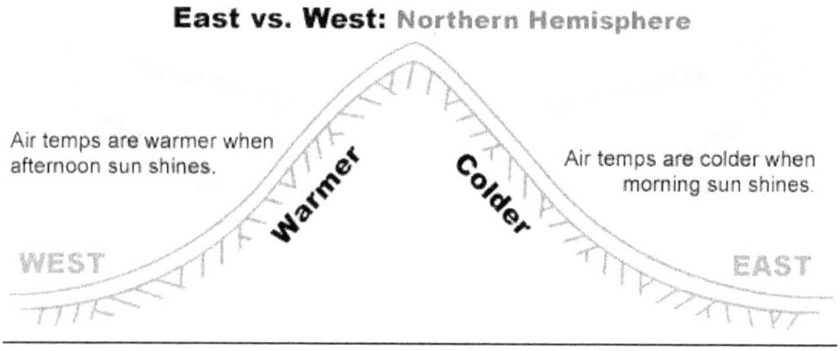

Fig. 2.11: Influence of aspect on temperature

Qn. *(1) "Climate of an area is determined by a number of factors". Discuss.*
(2) "Climate is the function of Interplay factors". Argue on this statement.

CHAPTER THREE

THE ATMOSPHERE

The atmosphere is the thin layer of gases, particulate matter and biotic matter held to the earth by gravitational attraction. Also the atmosphere can be defined as the gaseous envelop surrounding the earth. The atmosphere consists of different elements which can be recognized by differences in their densities and temperature according to altitude.

Have been believed that, the atmosphere was developed some millions of years ago and it is still maintaining its present form and composition as a result of chemical and photochemical process combined with differential escape rates from the earth's gravitational field. The atmosphere is held to the earth by the gravitational attraction of the earth and it is densest at the sea level and thin rapidly upwards.

Atmospheric Composition (Properties)
The atmosphere is composed by the following four (4) properties or composition:
1. Gaseous matter
2. Particulate matter
3. Biotic matter
4. Water vapor

1. Gaseous Matters (Principal Gases of Earth's Atmosphere)
Gaseous matters involve variety gases that are permanent and fixed in volume. The major gaseous matter in the atmosphere includes:

   a) Nitrogen (N_2) 78%
   b) Oxygen (O_2) 21%
   c) Carbon dioxide 0.03%
   d) Ozone 0.00006%
   e) Argon 0.93%

Others minor gases matter found in the atmosphere are as follows:

   a) Methane (CH_4) 0.00011%
   b) Sulphur dioxide (SO_2)
   c) Nitrogen dioxide (NO_2)

d) Helium (He) 0.0005%
e) Neon (Ne) 0.002%
f) Krypton (Kr) 0.00005%
g) Water Vapors (H_2O) 0.2 - 4.0%
h) Carbon Monoxide (Co)

Gaseous matters also can be grouped into the following four groups: 1. *Permanent or fixed gases* i.e. Nitrogen and Oxygen; 2. *Variable gases* i.e. Water vapor, Carbon dioxide and Ozone; 3. *Insert gases* i.e. Argon, Helium, Neone and Krypton; 4. *Pollutant gases* i.e. Nitrogen dioxide, Methane, Sulphur dioxide among others.

Gaseous matters are found in variant, minor amounts. Sulphur dioxide, Nitrogen dioxide, methane are pollutants which affiliates radiation and cause acidic rains.

In addition, most airs also contains minor between varying quantities of solid and liquid particle that can be thought of as impurities. The individual particles are mostly submicroscopic and therefore held in suspension on the air. Most air also contains some gaseous impurities (as smokes from industrial chimneys).

Pure air is invisible because the gases in it are colorless, *odorless,* and *tasteless.* Gaseous impurities, on the other hand, can often be smelled and the air may even become visible if enough submicroscopic solid and liquid impurities stick together to form particles large enough to either reflect or scatter sunlight. Clouds by far the most conspectus visible features of the atmosphere, represents simply a water vapor.

The amount of water vapor present determines the humidity of the atmosphere. It is most abundant in air overlying warm, most surface areas, such as tropical oceans, where water vapor may amount to as much 4% of total volume. Over deserts and in Polar Regions the amount of water vapor is a tiny fraction of 1%. Water vapor has a significant on *weather* and *climate* in that it is the source of all clouds and precipitation and is intimately involved in the storage, movement, and release of heat energy.

Atmospheric carbon dioxide also has a significant influence on climate, primarily because of its potential ability to absorb infrared radiation, which is the type of radiation that keeps the lower atmosphere warm. Carbon dioxide is distributed fairly uniformly in the lower layers of the atmosphere, but its

28

concentration has been increasing for the last century or so and the rate of accumulation has been accelerating presumably because of the increased burning of fossil fuels.

The long-range effects of the increased **burning** amounts of carbon dioxide in the atmosphere is debatable, but many scientists believe that the higher levels will cause the lower atmosphere to warm up enough to produce major, and still unpredictable, global changes.

Another minor, but vital gas in the atmosphere is **Ozone,** which is a molecule made up of three oxygen atoms joined together (0_3). For the most part, Ozone is concentrated in a layer of the atmosphere called the *Ozone layer*, which lies between *15km* and *48km* above the Earth's surface (but mostly between 15km and 20km). Ozone is an excellent absorber of ultraviolet solar radiation. It filters out enough of their rays to protect life forms from potentially deadly effects.

The other variable gases listed earlier as carbon monoxide, sulphur dioxide, nitrogen oxides and various hydrocarbons are increasingly being introduced into the atmosphere by emission from factories and automobiles. All of them may have some effects on climate (for example acid rains formation).

The atmosphere contains also **Particles.** The larger nongaseous particles in the atmosphere are mainly *water* and *ice*, which form clouds, rain, snow, sleet, and hail (frozen limps of water). These are also *dust particles*, large enough to be visible, which are sometimes kept aloft in the turbulent atmosphere in-sufficient quantity to cloud the sky (for example "dust storm" known well from Sahara or Australia). The particles of this dust are too heavy to remain long in the air.

Smaller particles invisible to the naked eye, solid or liquid, are called *Particulates*. They may remain suspend in the atmosphere for month. They have innumerable sources, some natural are from the result of human activities. Volcanic ash, wind-blow, soil and pollen grains, meteor debris, smoke from wild fires and salt spray from breaking waves are examples of particulates from natural sources. Particulates coming from human sources mostly consist of industrial and **automotive** emission and smoke from fires of human origin.

These tiny particles are most numerous near their places of origin-above cities, seacoast, and active Volcanoes. They may be carried great distances, both horizontally and vertically, by the restless atmosphere. They affect weather and climate in two major ways:

1. Many are hygroscopic (which means they absorb water), and water vapor condenses around them as they float about. This accumulation of water vapor molecules is a critical step in cloud formation.

2. Some either absorb or reflect sunlight, thus decreasing the amount of solar energy that reaches the earth's surface.

2. Particulate Matters.
These are sometimes known as *Aerosols*. They include dusts, ashes, Pollens, salt particles etc. These are very important in the atmosphere as they act as nuclei where water vapour collects during the formation of droplets through condensation and consequently formation of clouds then rainfall or precipitation. Their major functions are:
- (a) Absorption and reflection of solar radiation
- (b) Act as nuclei into which water vapors attack to form rain droplets and cloud and consequently rainfall.

3. Biotic Matters.
Biotic matters include all living organism which are suspended and floating in the atmosphere. These very small living organism are Bacteria, their influence is very minor and passing.

4. Water Vapor
Water vapor is the suspended liquid particle in the atmosphere. It comprises of 0.2-4% of the total atmospheric composition by volume. Water vapor plays important role in the atmosphere through:
- (a) Rain formation
- (b) Regulation of atmospheric temperature
- (c) Reflecting solar radiation.
- (d) They influence in weather and climate through reflects and absorbs solar radiation and hence maintains the so called atmospheric heat balance.

Importance (Effects) of Gaseous Matter in Weather and Climate:
(1) Nitrogen (N_2)
- - It is needed and used for plant growth
- - The impact is passive.

(2) Oxygen (O_2)
- Its effect on weather and climate since is needed by organism for respiration and the photosynthesis.
- It can be reduced through deforestation

(3) Carbon Dioxide (CO_2)
- Its effect on the atmosphere, absorb the incoming (short waves) solar radiation.
- It contributes too much green effects and consequently global warming.
- Used by plants for photosynthesis.

(4) Ozone layer (O_3)
- Refers to oxygen isotope with three isotopes
- Its major concentration is in stratosphere
- The major function is a filter of Ultra-violate rays.

The atmospheric Ozone Layer

The earth's atmosphere (stratosphere) contains ozone layer that contains three oxygen atoms which denoted as O_3. The lower region of stratosphere containing relatively concentration of ozone is called *Ozonosphere* which found between 15 to 35km (9 to 22 miles) above the surface of the earth. The average concentration of ozone in the atmosphere is around 0.6 parts per million. The highest concentrations of ozone occur at latitude from 26 to 28km in the tropics and from 12 to 20 km towards the poles.

The ozone layer was discovered in *1913* by the French Physicists called *Charles Fabry* and *Henri Buisson*. The ozone layer forms a thick layer in stratosphere, encircling the earth, which has large amount of ozone in it that act as the protection to the earth planet away from harmful radiations that comes from the sun. The ozone layer has the capability to absorb almost 97-99% of the harmful ultraviolet radiations that the sun emit and which can produce long term devastating effects on human beings as well as animals and plants.

Importance of Ozone Layer (Why Ozone Layer is Necessary?):
1. Essential properties of ozone molecules have an ability to block solar radiations of wavelengths less than *290 nanometers* from reaching earth's surface.

2. It also absorbs ultraviolet radiations that are dangerous for most living beings. Ultraviolet radiations could injure or kill life on earth through the absorption of ultraviolet radiations warms the stratosphere but it is important for life to flourish on planet earth.

Ozone Layer Depletion

Ozone depletion occurs when destruction of the stratospheric ozone is more than the production of the molecule. The scientists have observed reduction in stratospheric ozone since early of 1970s. It is more prominent in Polar Regions and mid-latitudes that led to the formation of *ozone holes* or *atmospheric windows*. Ozone holes refer to the regions of severely reduced ozone layers. The following are some of the *causes of ozone layer depletion:*

1. *Natural causes of depletion of ozone layer:* ozone layer has been found to be affected by certain natural phenomena such as sun-spots and atmospheric winds. This has been found to cause not 1-2% depletion of the ozone layer and the effects are also thought to be only temporary. It is also believed that the *volcanic eruptions* have also contributed towards ozone depletion through adding destructive gases to the ozone layer.

2. *Man-made causes of ozone layer depletion:* the main causes are determined to the excessive release of *chlorine* and *bromine* from man-made compounds such as chlorofluorocarbons (CFCs). CFCs (Chlorofluorocarbons), halons, CH_3CCl_3 (Methyl chloroform), CCl_4 (Carbon tetrachloride), HCFCs (Hydro-chlorofluorocarbons), hydro-bromofluorocarbons and methyl bromide are found have direct impact on the depletion of the ozone layer. These are categorized as Ozone-Depleting Substances (ODS).

   Chlorofluorocarbons are released into the atmosphere due to: cleaning agents, packing materials, coolants in refrigerators, air conditioning and aerosol spray cans. ODS are not washed back in the form of rain on the earth, they remain in the atmosphere for a quite a long time then are transported into the stratosphere. ODS accounts for nearly 90% of total depletion of ozone layer in stratosphere through destroying molecular structure of ozone layer. Main Ozone Depleting Substances (ODS):

* Chlorofluorocarbons account for more than 80% of ozone depletion. Used in freezers, air cooling components, dry-cleaning agents, hospital sterilants.
* Methyl Chloroform used for vapor degreasing, some aerosols, cold cleaning, adhesives and chemical processing.
* Carbon Tetrachloride mainly used in fire extinguishers
* Hydro-chlorofluorocarbons are substitutes for CFC's but still play a vital role in ozone depletions.

Effect of Ozone Layer Depletion:

1. Disruption of susceptible terrestrial and aquatic ecosystems due to depletion of ozone layer. Ultraviolet radiations could destroy organic matters hence plants and plankton cannot thrive, both acts as food for land and sea animals respectively. Death and disappearance of some plants and animal species also is due to the adverse atmospheric changes caused by the impact of ultraviolet radiations.

2. Ozone layer depletion lead to the melting of ice due to the increase of temperature which caused by strong rays coming direct from the sun that reach the surface of the earth without being filtered in the stratosphere.

3. For humans, excessive exposure to ultraviolet radiations leads to higher risks of cancer (especially skin cancer) and cataracts. It is calculated that every 1% decrease in ozone layer results in a 2-5% increase in the occurrence of skin cancer.

4. Influence to the rise of sea level due to the melting of ice on the surface of the earth that caused by creation of ozone holes over which allows the free penetration of ultraviolet rays.

Trial Questions.
(1) Examine the effects of different components of the atmosphere on the weather and climate.
(2) Describe and explain the composition of the atmosphere.
(3)Discuss for the positive (significance) and negative effects of the atmosphere.

Vertical Structure of the Atmosphere

Atmosphere refers to an envelope of the earth's crust which is held above the earth's surface with the influence of gravitation. Vertical structure of the atmosphere is also known as vertical section of the atmosphere or layered structure of the atmosphere. The atmosphere consists of different materials and layers of different amount of densities and characteristics such as temperature and moisture. According to the *International Conversion*, the atmospheric characteristic explained as:

(1) Most of atmospheric conditions such as weather and climate concentration are within 10km along the equator and 8km at the poles.
(2) 50% of atmospheric masses are found within 5.6km above the Earth's surface.
(3) 99% of atmospheric masses are found within 40km above the Earth's surface.
(4) The furthest limit of the atmosphere is said to go a little bit by 1000km.

Division (Layers) Of the Vertical Structure of the Atmosphere

The divisions of the vertical structure of the atmosphere are classified basing on three (3) major criteria:
(1) According to thermal temperature change
(2) According to Physiochemical composition
(3) According to turbulence of gases or winds.

In this book, we shall discuss much in the classification of vertical structure of the atmosphere according to *thermal temperature change*. Vertical structure of the atmosphere according to *thermal temperature change* involves the variation of temperature in relation to altitude that has been categorized into five (5) layers:

(a) Troposphere   (d) Thermosphere
(b) Stratosphere   (e) Exosphere
(c) Mesosphere

A. TROPOSPHERE.

Troposphere refers to the first lowest bottom layer in the atmosphere. It may reach to about 16/17km from the earth's surface along the Equator and 8km at or around the Poles.

In this zone, there is vertical and horizontal movement of air. Here also temperature tends to decrease with the increase in height above sea level (altitude) at the average of 0.6°C per 100m (6°c per 1000m). The rate at which temperature decreases with the increase in altitude is known as *Environmental lapse rate* (ELR).

About 80% of atmospheric gases, water vapor, dusts, and pollutants are concentrated in this layer. Also different wind system (are unstable) and clouds occurs in this zone. The upper limit of the layer is known as *tropopause* where temperatures remain constant. The troposphere is very importance base at least all of the weather and climate conditions occur in this layer.

B. STRATOSPHERE (OZONOSPHERE)

This is the second layer which extends to about 17km to 50km from the earth's surface. In this, lower part, temperature is about -50°C and it is constant. This part (lower part of the stratosphere) is also known as *Isothermal layer.*

The layer is characterized by stead increase of temperature with the increase of altitude as known as *Temperature inversion.* Temperature inversion is the tendency of temperature to increase with the increase in altitude which is influenced by presence of Ozone layer. The Ozone layer in this layer contributes much to the rapid increase in temperature. Maximum concentration of ozone layer at the height is (between) 25 to 30km.

The upper limit of this layer (stratosphere) is called *Stratopause* where the temperature remains constant. The wind in this layer is lighter at lower part but increase with heights. The Ozone layer found in the stratosphere is very important because it reflects and absorbs the incoming ultra-violet radiation from the sun. By so doing it regulates the temperature of the earth.

The troposphere and stratosphere from the lower atmosphere they are separated from one another by thin layer of discontinuity called *Tropopause.*

C. MESOSPHERE

This is the third layer separated from the stratosphere by the layer (zone) of discontinuity known as *Stratopause.* Mesosphere extends to about 80km or 90km above the earth's surface. In this layer temperature falls rapidly because, there is no dusts, water vapor, cloud cover or ozone to absorb incoming solar radiation. This layer is coldest in the atmosphere in which the temperature decreases to about – 90°C or -100°C at its top (upper limit). The strongest of the speed of the wind is about 3000km/hr. is experienced. The upper limit of this layer is called *Mesopause.*

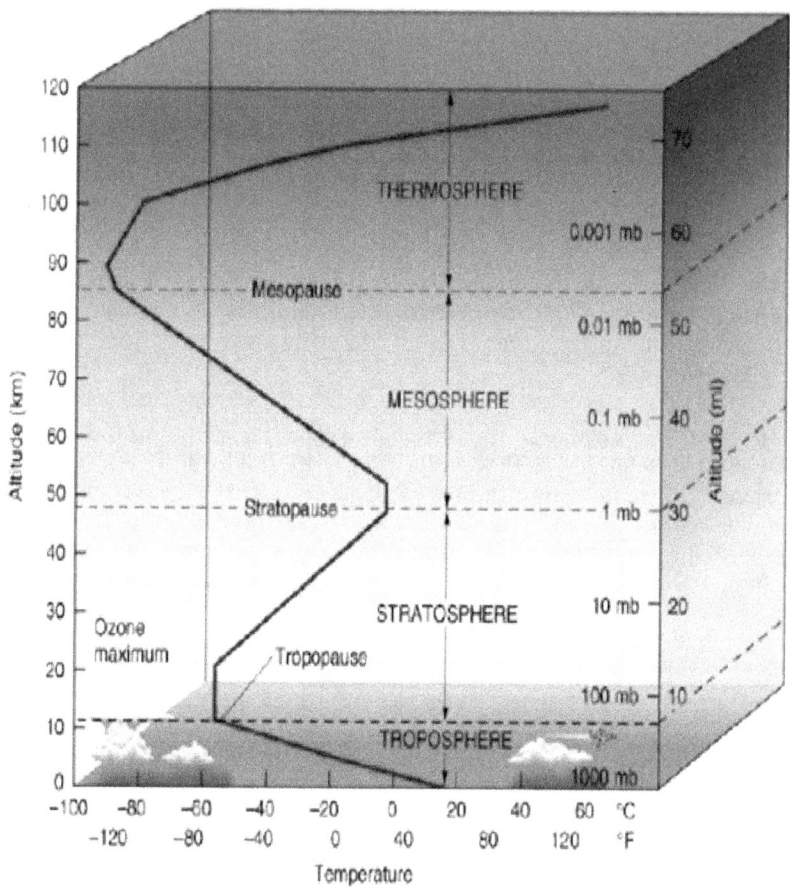

Fig. 3.1: Vertical structure of the atmosphere.

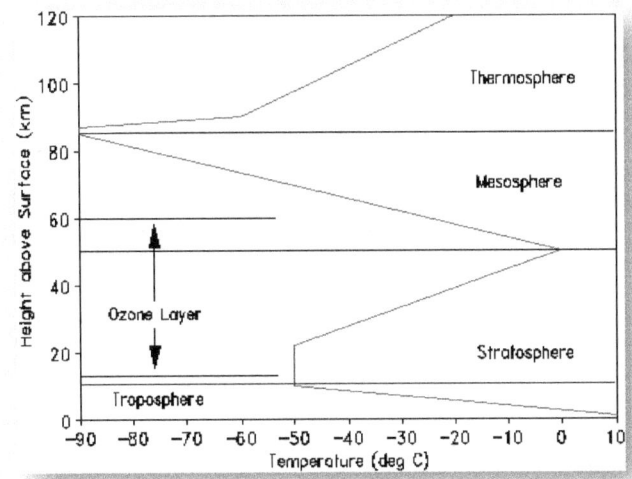

Fig. 3.2: Vertical structure of the atmosphere

D. THERMOSPHERE (IONOSPHERE)

This is the fourth layer in the atmosphere which is separated from Mesosphere by the zone of discontinuity known as **Mesopause.** It extends from 75km to 100km (46 to 62 miles) direct below the Exosphere. The temperature in this zone is rapidly increased with the increase in altitude. The temperature reaches to about 1500°C. The increase in temperature in this layer is caused by the presence of electronically charged ions and free electrons which absorb and reflect radio short waves of the sunrays.

Here also there is atomic Oxygen which absorbs solar energy. In the Thermosphere, there is another layer called *Ionosphere* in which electro-magnetic waves including radio signals are reflected back to the earth's surface and facilitate wireless communication. Only half of the earth's ionosphere is being ionized by the Sun at any time.

E. EXOSPHERE

Exosphere refers to the last layer in the atmospheric vertical structure which reaches beyond 960Km (or about 1000Km) from the earth's surface. It reaches and extends to the interplanetary space. This zone is extremely dark and has not been much investigated.

General Positive Impact or Effect of the Atmosphere

a. The atmosphere provides light and heat needed by all living organism, especially light is needed by plants to manufacture food through photosynthesis.

b. It provides oxygen that inhaled by all living organisms.

c. The atmospheric circulation leads to the formation of rain and other forms of precipitation hence lead to the availability of moisture and water on the earth's surface.

d. The atmosphere supports communication through transmissions of human sounds that makes hearing possible.

e. The atmospheric circulation that leads to the formation of precipitation (especially rains) may cause for the generation of Hydro Electric Power (HEP) due to the formation of water falls.

f. The ozone layer that held in the atmosphere, protects living organism from dangerous radiations from the sun.

g. The atmosphere also acts as the blanket of the earth by preserving heat that keeps the earth planet warmly.

h. Clouds in the atmosphere reflect insolation back into space preventing the occurrence of high temperature on the earth's surface.

i. In the atmosphere, air movement enables airplanes, birds and insects to fly from one place to another.

j. The ionosphere, that held in the atmosphere, supports radio waves communication to distant places.

k. Wind movement in the atmosphere, supports distribution of rainfall to the earth's surface.

l. The atmosphere facilitates to the development of tourism due to the ice formation that caused by extreme cooling of the atmosphere.

m. Gases or airs that held in the atmosphere burns all meteorites that might cause loss of lives and destruction of properties on the earth's surface.

General Negative Impact or Effect of the Atmosphere

a. Storms in the atmosphere that caused by violent air circulation, leads to the destruction of houses and hindrance in air transport.

b. Atmospheric storms wind storms destruct crops in farms and occurrence of flood along coastal areas.

c. Scarcity of water vapor in the atmosphere leads to the droughts that may cause formation of famine, death of plants and animals.

d. Pollution of the atmosphere may cause to the formation of acidic rains that tends to destroy soil, crops, vegetation cover and other living organisms.

e. Pollution to the atmosphere also leads to the occurrence of diseases like bronchitis and skin itching.

f. Electric charges in the atmosphere that produced during the thunderstorms formation leads to destruction of property and death of people and animals.

g. An extreme cold condition in the atmosphere leads to the soil freezing, human disconformity, frost that tend to affect agricultural activities.

h. Mist and fog hinder the effectiveness of cars movement and sometimes may cause to the occurrence of accidents.

i. Frequent high rainfall from the atmosphere leads to soil erosion and floods. These floods tend to destroy the soil fertility and cause deaths to living organism.

ENERGY IN THE ATMOSPHERE (INSOLATION)

The sun is the main source of heat in the atmosphere although there are some other (minor) sources such as volcanoes, industries, domestic activities etc. The *radiated heat* from the sun is the major source of energy. The earth receives heat energy as the *incoming short waves* solar radiation from the sun. These short waves are radiated and pass through the atmosphere towards the earth's surface.

As the heat energy passes the atmosphere some of it, is absorbed and reflected back into space before reaching the earth's surface. It is the only part of the solar energy generates many gases to reach and being received by earth's surface and this is what we call *insolation*. Generally, the earth's surface receives heat energy from three ways (basic sources). These include:

- ☑ Solar radiation
- ☑ Gravity (gravitational force) and
- ☑ Androgenic force coming from within the earth.

But the most significant source of heat energy is solar radiation which transmitted from sun in a form of short waves travelling at the rate of 186, 000 miles per second; in other way, incoming solar radiation travels about 150 million kilometers from the sun to the earth's surface within $8\frac{1}{2}$ minutes (except for small amount of energy).

What is insolation?

(a) Insolation is the amount of solar energy received at the earth's surface.

(b) It is the solar energy sent into or radiated which reaches the earth's surface in the form of short waves.

(c) It is the energy that controls our plants, weather and climate conditions and also supports all kind of life.

Distribution of Insolation (The Global Pattern Insolation)

The amount of insolation reaching the earth's surface is not even distributed around the world. The amount of insolation received at the earth's surface decrease from the equator towards the poles but there is temperature variation of insolation received at different latitude at different time of the year. The globe is divided into three zones on the basis of the amount of insolation received in a year. The followings are the places where insolation is distributed globally:

1. Low Latitude or Tropical Zone

This zone extends between the tropics of Cancer and Capricorn. Every place receives maximum and minimum insolation twice a year. The following map illustrates the global distribution of insolation reaching the earth's surface.

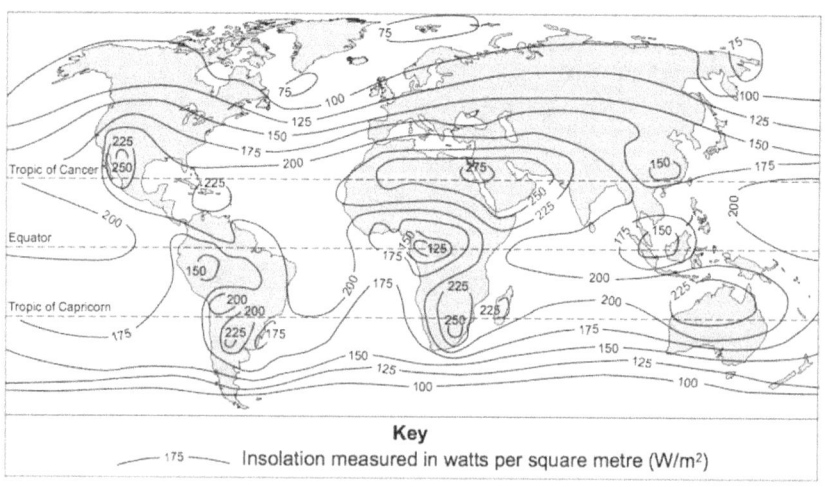

Key

—175— Insolation measured in watts per square metre (W/m²)

Fig.3.3: Global distribution of insolation

2. Middle Latitude

This zone found between 23½⁰ and 66½⁰ latitudes in both of hemisphere of the earth planet. Within this zone, every place receives maximum insolation during summer and minimum insolation during winter.

3. Polar Zone

This zone found between 66⁰ and 90⁰ pole latitudes in both of hemisphere of the earth planet. Polar zones also receive maximum and minimum insolation but sometimes insolation is between zero (0) due to the absence of direct solar rays.

Factors Affecting (Influencing) Distribution (Variation) of Insolation

The actual amount of insolation received at a place on the earth varies according to the conditions of the atmosphere as well as the seasons. The following are astronomical and geographical factors govern the amount of insolation received at any point on the earth's surface:

1. *Angle of the sun rays and Altitude of the sun (Angle of incidence):* The angle between the sun rays and the target to the surface of the earth at a given point largely determines the amount of insolation received. Insolation in the maximum area receives vertical sun rays; this is because these rays characterized by spreading and heating over minimum area. On the other hand region received an oblique sun rays normally experience minimum insolation.

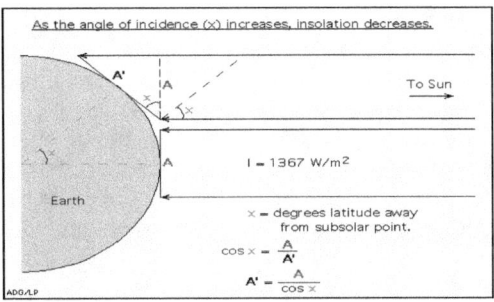

Fig.3.4: Angle of incidence

In the other words, if the angle of the sun rays decreases pole wards also the amount of insolation received in an area tends to decrease pole wards. As the

41

angle of the sun rays heating the earth, decreases the amount of insolation lost through absorption and reflection increases, thus; areas at low altitudes receive high insolation than those at high altitude.

2. *Length of day (Duration of the sunshine):* The length of day varies at all places except at the equator. The longer the duration of sunshine and the shorter duration of night maximum the amount of insolation received at the earth's surface. On the other hand the shorter the duration of sunshine and the longer the period of night the less the amount of insolation.

3. *Distance between the earth and the sun:* Since the earth revolves around the sun in an elliptical orbit, the distance varies during the course of a year. The mean distance between the earth and sun is about 149,000,000 kilometers. Each year, on January 3rd, the earth comes closer to the sun about a distance of 147 million kilometers. This position is known as *perihelion*. On July 4th, the earth is little farther from the sun when the distance becomes about 152 million kilometers. This position is called *aphelion*.

The earth at the time of perihelion (nearest to the sun 147Km) should receive maximum insolation while at the time of aphelion (furthest from the sun 152Km) earth's surface should receive minimum insolation. Although the amount of incoming solar radiation received at the outer boundary of the atmosphere is a little greater (7 percent) in January than in July, there are other major factors, such as the angle of incidence and the duration of sunshine that more than offset its effect on seasonal temperature variations. It may be interesting to note that the earth is relatively closer to the sun during the northern hemisphere winter.

4. *Sun spots due to burning of helium (Solar constant).* Sun spots are created in the solar outer surface due to periodic disturbances and explosion. The number of sun spots at the sun ray increase from year to year (normally every 11 years). The increase of energy radiation from the sun tends to increase the number of spots in the sun. The scientists give opinion that the number of sunspots increases or decreases on a regular basis, creating a cycle of 11 years. However, on the effect caused by sun spots, there is little doubt that the magnitude of the effects of the varying amount of the solar constant on the amount of solar radiation received here on earth seems to be too small.

5. *Effect of the atmosphere:* Incoming solar radiation had to pass this layer of the earth's atmosphere. So, during this transmission part, solar radiation absorbed partly reflected and partly scattered by the atmosphere. Absorption

is equal to 14% that absorbed by atmospheric gases like ozone, oxygen, and carbon dioxide, also water vapor and scattering of solar radiation by the dust particles in the atmosphere is equal to 23%.

6. The elevation above the sea level (The height above the sea level): As the height above the sea level increase, insolation decreases and vice versa. This is because: Firstly the atmosphere is not directly heated by the sun, but by the heat reflected from the earth's surface and distributed through conduction and convection. Secondly also at high altitude the density of air heated pressure decreases, thus its ability to hold heat decreases too because here there are fewer molecules and particles which are very widely spaced

7. *The density and pressure of the air:* As the density or pressure of the air decreases, its ability to hold heat decrease, this is because; the molecules in the air that receive and retain heat become fewer and more widely spaced.

8. *Nature of the land and sea (nature of the earth's surface):* The Sea is capable of absorbing heat to the depth of about 10m and it is capable of transmitting that heat to more depth through currents and waves than the land. The sea also has higher *specific heat capacity* (S.H.C) than land i.e. S.H.C of Water = 4.2KJ/Kg°C. S.H.C of clay Soil = 2.1KJ/Kg°C, and SHC of Sand Soil = 0.8 KJ/Kg°C

9. *Prevailing winds:* The temperature of the wind is determined by its source, region and by the characteristics of the surface over which it blows. Thus winds blow in the sea tend to be warmer in winter and cooler in summer than those blowing from the landmass.

10. *Seasonal changes:* During springs and autumn equinox; September 22nd and March 21st, when the sun is directly overhead at the equator, the rate of insolation is distributed equally between both hemispheres. During summer and winter solstices; 21st June and 22nd December when the sun is overhead at tropics, the hemisphere experiencing summer, will receive more insolation than the one experiencing winter.

11. *Ocean currents:* The ocean currents play a great role in the horizontal heat transfer (sea heat budget). Warmer ocean currents raise the temperature of the air and consequently the surrounding land mass hence maximum insolation. The reverses true about cool ocean currents tend to cool the air temperature and the surrounding land mass hence minimum insolation.

12. Length of day and night: Insolation is only received during day light hours and reaches into maximum (peak) at noon. Along the equator there is no seasonal variation of the insolation because the days and nights are always equal. The polar areas receives insolation during part of winter when there is continuous insolation received, but many receives up to 24 hours insolation in a part of summer when there continuous day light.

13. *Cloud cover:* The presence of clouds reduces both incoming and outgoing solar energy radiation. Clouds may reduce day time temperature but they also act   as *insulating blankets* which protect the outgoing heat in the night, thus; the thicker the clouds, the greater the amounts of absorption, reflection and scattering of insolation. This explains the reasons as to why:

    i.   Tropical deserts are warmer during day and cooler in the nights, because there are cloudless.
    ii.   Humid equatorial regions which have cloud covers have very low temperature variation between day and night.

14. Aspect: In the northern hemisphere, the north facing slopes are in shadow in most time while south facing slopes receive more insolation as they do face the sun rays. In contrast, in the southern hemisphere the south facing slopes receive more insolation than the north facing slopes.

15. Urbanization: This alters albedo and creates the so called *'urban'* heat *'islands'* i.e.:

    (i)   Large cities generate more dusts and condensation nuclei than the natural environment.
    (ii)   The buildings and materials used in large cities absorb heat during the day time.
    (iii)   Dark-colored roofs, concretes, block walls and tarmac roads have high capacity of absorbing and retaining heat during the day time and retaining heat during the day time and release it slowly in the night.
    (iv)   In towns heat is also generated from car fumes, factories, power stations, homes etc.
    (v)   Tower buildings and other concentrated buildings in towns or large cities tend to break the moving winds which are responsible for distribution of heat horizontally and vertically.

Thus; one can conclude that, under normal circumstances, temperature are warmest in the more built-up centres and decrease towards sub-urban and open country side.

16. Solar inputs: Solar input refers to the intensity of the insolation emitted from the sun which is later received at the outer limit of the atmosphere. The measure of the intensity of the insolation received at the outer limit of the atmosphere is called *solar constant.* Variation in the solar input leads to the variation of insolation received on the earth's surface depending on the increase or decrease.

Modification of Solar Radiation in The Atmosphere
The atmosphere modifies the solar radiation through the following process:

1. *Absorption:* solar radiation affected (absorbed) by water vapor, clouds, carbon dioxide, ozone, aerosols and other gases. About 21% of solar radiation reduced through absorption.

2. *Reflection:* about 24% of solar radiation is reflected back from both the atmosphere and the ground. Reflection depends on the nature of the surface. Percentage of solar energy reflected back (reflection coefficient) is called *albedo.* On white and shiny surfaces, albedo is higher than in dark surfaces. Clouds are greater reflectors due to having higher albedo caused by white and shiny top surfaces.

3. *Scattering:* about 9% of solar energy is depleted before reaching the surface. Scattering involves transferring of energy in all directions in which caused by air molecules and dust particles. Scattering is also known as *diffuse reflection.* Scattered radiation is not converted into heat energy. Scattering have the following types:

   (a) *Mie scattering:* takes place when diameter of particle is larger than the wavelengths of the incident rays. It is non-selective but effective for all wavelengths.

   (b) *Rayleigh scattering:* takes place when the diameter of the particles is smaller than the wavelengths of incident solar radiation.

It is important to note that, only about 46% (balance) of solar energy reaches the earth's surface that is converted to heat energy.

Earth Albedo
The word *albedo* (or reflection coefficient*)* derived from Latin word (albedo or for white) which means **"whiteness"** or **"reflected sunlight"** in turn from *albus* **"white".** By definition, **albedo** is the ratio between incoming solar

radiation and the amount of solar radiation reflected back into space expressed in percentage. **Earth albedo** is the capacity of a surface to reflect the solar radiation or energy. The earth albedo involves scatting, reflection and absorption of solar energy.

In other words, albedo can be expressed as the ratio between the total solar energy (radiation) filling upon a surface and the amount reflected expresses as a decimal or percentage. For example the earth's average albedo (including also albedo of the clouds) is about 0.4% (0.4% i.e. 4/10 of solar radiation is reflected into space). Therefore, temperature is markedly higher for a place with low albedo than of the place with high albedo.

Land and water surface for example have quite different characteristics. Water has tendency to store heat that it receives while the land quickly returns (reflects) it to the atmosphere. On the other hand this experience, land has greater albedo or reflective capacity than water surface. The Earth albedo tends to form different surface: dark soil 0.03%, Snow field 0.8%, water 0.02%, grass land 0.25%.

Main Factors Affecting Earth Albedo

As you have seen that, temperature is markedly higher for a place with low albedo than of the place with high albedo; therefore, albedo is highly affected by the following factors:

i. *Types of clouds.* For example:
    (a) It is 30% - 40% in the thinner clouds such as cirrus clouds.
    (b) It is 50% - 79% in the thicker-clouds such as stratus.
    (c) It is 90% in the thickest clouds such as cumulo-nimbus.

ii. *Land surfaces.* For example:
    (a) It is less than 10% over ocean and dark soil.
    (b) It is about 15% over coniferous forests and urban areas.
    (c) It is 25% over grass lands and deciduous forests.
    (d) It is 40% over light-clouded deserts.
    (e) It is 85% over fresh snow.

Note: Albedo increases as deforestation and overgrazing occurs. This reduces the possibility of clouds and rainfall formation, hence increases the possibilities of desertification to occur.

Heat Budget (Heat Energy) On the Earth and Atmosphere.

Heat budget is the balance between the amount of solar radiation received by the earth's surface and its atmosphere and the amount of heat lost from the earth by outgoing terrestrial long wave radiation from earth's surface and lost heat from atmosphere. Heat budget is the distribution of heat from the sun to the earth's surface and its approximation is about 6, 000°C.

Earth's net radiation, sometimes called *net flux*, is the balance between incoming and outgoing energy at the top of the atmosphere. It is the total energy that is available to influence the climate. Energy comes into the system when insolation penetrates the top of the atmosphere. Energy goes out in two ways: reflection by clouds, aerosols, or the earth's surface; and thermal radiation when heat emitted by the surface and the atmosphere, including clouds. The global average net radiation must be close to zero over the span of a year or else the average temperature will rise or fall.

In short, as insolation enters the atmosphere in the form of short wave ultraviolet light, it interacts with atmospheric elements. Roughly, 46 percent of insolation reaches the Earth's surface. The rest is both reflected and scattered back to space through its interaction with clouds, water vapour, dust and pollen, known collectively as *aerosols* or it is absorbed by clouds and gaseous elements and hence heats the atmosphere. Insolation reaching the surface of the earth is used to warm it up. The earth's surface then heats up the overlying atmosphere through transfers of *sensible heat, latent heat* and the release of *long-wave radiation.*

Conduction is when heat is conducted from the ground to the air that is in direct contact with the ground. The air, which is warmed by conduction, then rises by *convection* because it is less dense than the air around it. In this way heat is transferred into the upper parts of the atmosphere. *Latent heat transfer* energy is required to evaporate water into a vapor.

Therefore, the energy that was required to evaporate the water is stored within the vapor as *latent heat.* The vapor then rises into the atmosphere through convection, or through forced rise (along fronts or up mountains) or by turbulence. On condensation the latent heat is released into the atmosphere as sensible heat, which warms the atmosphere.

Long-wave radiation is the energy radiating from the earth as infrared radiation at low energy to space. Once in the atmosphere, gases and liquids absorb the long-wave radiation. The diagram and animation below illustrate the Earth's average heat budget.

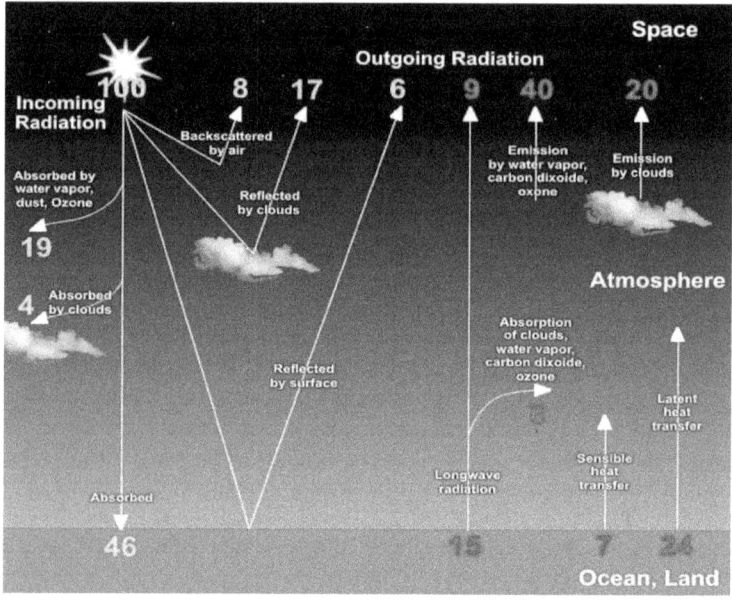

Fig.3.5: Heat budget

The Global Redistribution of Heat

There is an alarming imbalance of net radiation between the polar and tropical regions. To maintain a balance across the world, heat is transferred by three main methods:

Ocean currents
Warm ocean currents move heat from the tropics to the poles while cold ocean currents work in the opposite direction.

Trade winds
These transfer large amounts of heat from the tropics to the poles.

Storms
Tropical cyclones transfer large amounts of heat energy from the tropics (where they develop) to the subtropics and temperate zones.

Influential Factors of Heat Energy Distribution to the Atmosphere:

1. *Nature of the surface*: nature of the surface differs in term of specific heat capacities and albedo. *Specific heat capacity* defined as the number of calories required to raise the temperature of 1 gram of that substance through 1°C. Some surfaces have higher albedo than others and higher specific heat capacities than others which have low specific heat capacities. All these variation affects the value of insolation. Water absorbs more insolation and stores it but land reflects more radiant energy due to its high albedo.

2. *Latitudinal location*: affects the amount of insolation, both duration of daylight and distance travelled by the solar radiation through the atmosphere to the earth's surface.

3. *Elevation and aspect:* elevation is the land altitude while aspect is the direction where the slope faces in relation to solar insolation. Solar radiation received by surface of the earth is also controlled by the elevation and aspect. Some slopes are more exposed to solar radiation than others, and then they receive more insolation.

The Difference between Heat and Temperature

By definition, **heat** is the amount of energy in a body, but **temperature** is the measure of the intensity of heat. The comparison and contrast between heat and temperature can be drawn clearly on the following grounds:

1. Heat is nothing but the amount of energy in a body. As against this, temperature is something that measures the intensity of heat.

2. Heat measures both kinetic and potential energy contained by molecules in an object. On the other hand, temperature measures average kinetic energy of molecules in substance.

3. The main feature of heat is that it travels from hotter region to cooler region. Unlike temperature, which rises when heated and falls when cooled.

4. Heat possesses the ability to work, but the temperature is used exclusively to gauge the extent of heat.

5. The standard unit of measurement of heat is Joules, while that of temperature is Kelvin, but it can also be measured in Celsius and Fahrenheit.

6. Calorimeter is a device, which is used to measure the heat. On the other hand, temperature can be measured by thermometer.

7. Heat is represented by 'Q' whereas 'T' is used to represent temperature.

Basic Comparison	Heat	Temperature
Meaning	Heat is the amount of energy in a body.	Temperature is the measure of the intensity of heat.
Measures	Total kinetic and potential energy contained by molecules in an object.	Average kinetic energy of molecules in a substance.
Property	Flows from hotter object to cooler object.	Rises when heated and falls when cooled.
Working ability	Yes	No
Unit of measurement	Joules	Kelvin
Device	Calorimeter	Thermometer
Labelled as	Q	T

Table 3.1: Basic comparison between heat and temperature

Vertical Variation of Temperature and Lapse Rate

Lapse rate refers to the situation where by temperature decrease with the increase in altitude or increase with the decrease of altitude. It is also, the rate of change of temperature with the change of altitude.

Temperature Inversion

Temperature inversion is an increase in temperature with height, or to the layer (inversion layer) within which such an increase occurs. Therefore; temperature inversion simply can be defined as increasing of temperature with increasing height or altitude above the earth's surface.

Temperature inversion is also called *negative lapse rate*. This phenomenon may occur near the earth's surface or at great height in the atmosphere. The rate of change of temperature with altitude in temperature inversion is called *reversed lapse rate* or *abnormal lapse rate*.

Inversions play an important role in determining cloud forms, precipitation, and visibility. An inversion acts as a cap on the upward movement of air from the layers below. As a result, convection produced by the heating of air from below is limited to levels below the inversion.

50

Diffusion of dust, smoke, and other air pollutants is likewise limited. In regions where a pronounced low-level inversion is present, convective clouds cannot grow high enough to produce showers and, at the same time, visibility may be greatly reduced below the inversion, even in the absence of clouds, by the accumulation of dust and smoke particles. Because air near the base of an inversion tends to be cool, fog is frequently present there.

Inversions also affect diurnal variations in air temperature. The principal heating of air during the day is produced by its contact with a land surface that has been heated by the Sun's radiation. Heat from the ground is communicated to the air by conduction and convection. Since an inversion will usually control the upper level to which heat is carried by convection, only a shallow layer of air will be heated if the inversion is low and large, and the rise in temperature will be great.

Inversions also affect diurnal variations in air temperature. The principal heating of air during the day is produced by its contact with a land surface that has been heated by the Sun's radiation. Heat from the ground is communicated to the air by *conduction* and *convection*. Since an inversion will usually control the upper level to which heat is carried by convection, only a shallow layer of air will be heated if the inversion is low and large, and the rise in temperature will be great.

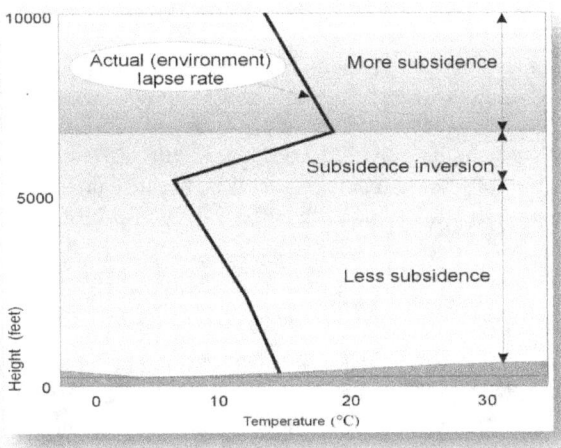

Fig.3.6: Temperature inversion

Temperature inversion is very common in the *stratosphere* and *thermosphere*. However temperature inversion can occur even near the ground and high in the troposphere. Some of the temperature inversions last for short time, for example *nocturnal temperature inversions* while other stay for long time, for example *subsidence (high level) temperature inversions.*

Other temperature inversions occurring at high altitude are referred to as *high level temperature inversion.* High level inversion is commonly found in depressions where warm air masses over rides cold air masses at the warm front.

Effects of Temperature Inversion

As we have seen that, temperature inversion is as increasing of temperature with increasing height or altitude above the earth's surface. Therefore, temperature inversion has some of the following effects:

(a) Temperature inversions play an important role in determining cloud forms, precipitation and visibility.

(b) An inversion of temperature acts as a cap on the upward movement of air from the layers below. As a result, convection produced by the heating of air from below is **limited** to levels below the inversion. **Diffusion** of dust, smoke, and other air pollutants is likewise limited.

(c) In regions where a pronounced low-level inversion is present, convective clouds **cannot** grow high enough to produce showers.

(d) Visibility may be greatly reduced below the inversion due to the accumulation of dust and smoke particles. Because air near the base of an inversion tends to be cool, **fog** is frequently present there.

(e) Inversions also affect diurnal variations in temperature. Diurnal variations tend to be very **small**.

(f) An inversion can lead to pollution such as smog being trapped close to the ground, with possible adverse effects on health. An inversion can also suppress convection by acting as a "cap". If this cap is broken for any of several reasons, convection of any moisture present can then erupt into violent thunderstorms.

(g) Temperature inversion can notoriously result in freezing rain in cold climates. Temperatures in troposphere normally decrease with increasing height or over age of 0.6°C per 100m (as warm lapse rate). But sometimes this normal trend of decreasing of temperature with increasing heights is reversed due to special circumstances.

Ideal Conditions for Temperature Inversion

The following are the conditions for temperature inversion to occur:

(a) Long nights, so that the outgoing radiation is greater than the incoming radiation.
(b) Clear skies, which allow unobstructed escape of radiation.
(c) Calm and stable air, so that there is no vertical mixing at lower levels.
(d) When the two air masses of different meteorological characteristics meet whereby the warm air is forced to rise.
(e) When warm air moves over a cool surface of landmass or ocean

Causes of Temperature Inversion

The following are some of the causes of temperature inversion:

i. *Radiation,* (of infra-red energy) that it is caused by the use of energy on the earth's surface that makes the ground to cool abruptly.

ii. *Air subsidence* caused by the friction between airs leading to the production of temperature. This occurs during downward movement of air.

iii. *Formations of fronts,* if it takes place where two air masses with different characteristics of temperature meet. On the meeting, the warm air is alone on cold air.

iv. *Advection,* it takes place when warm air passes over and horizontally leaving the upper portion warmer due to being far from the surface. Refers to the fog.

v. *Water vapor,* this keeps temperature for a long time hence keeps the atmosphere warmer than near the surface.

vi. *Presence of ozone layer* in the atmosphere also cause for the temperature inversion. The ozone in the atmosphere absorbs energy from the sun hence the reaction between ultraviolet rays and the ozone gives off heat in which warms the atmosphere and not the atmosphere

Types of Temperature Inversion

Types of temperature inversions are based on the *level of occurrence* (ground level and high level) and their causes or genetic (subsidence, advection, radiation and frontal). Therefore, there are five kinds of inversions as explained:

1. Advection inversion:

Advection inversion is influenced by warmer air mass advancing across the cold surface. The lower gets cold while the upper part remains warm. This can be over the colder sea in summer or over the land mass in winter.

2. Ground inversion (Ground surface temperature inversion):

It is formed when ground surface becomes cold during winter in night due to excessive loss of heat in the form of long wave terrestrial radiation. The above layer of air come into the contact with cold ground is relatively warm. Consequently temperature inversion develops. Ground surface inversion also called **radiation** or **nocturnal** inversion.

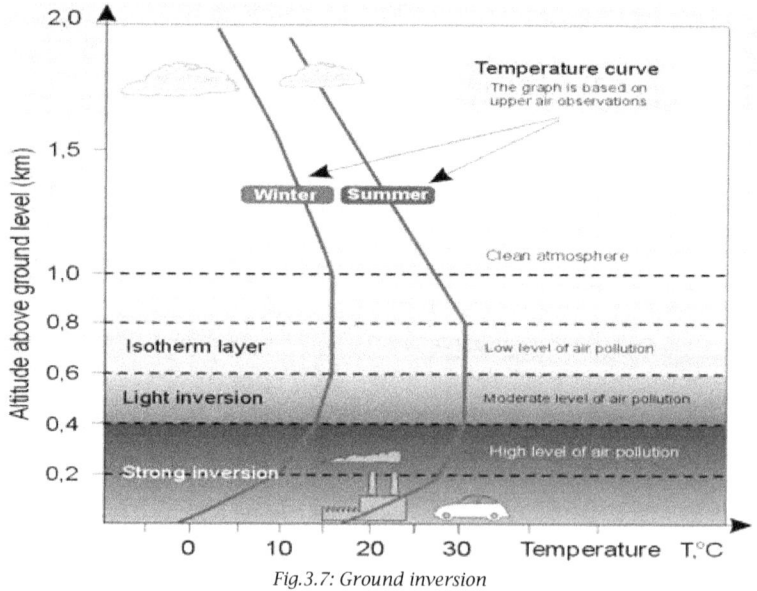

Fig.3.7: Ground inversion

A ground inversion develops when air is cooled by contact with a colder surface until it becomes cooler than the overlying atmosphere; this occurs most often on clear nights, when the ground cools off rapidly by radiation. If the temperature of surface air drops below its dew point, fog may result. Topography greatly affects the magnitude of ground inversions. If the land is rolling or hilly, the cold air formed on the higher land surfaces tends to drain into the hollows, producing a larger and thicker inversion above low ground and little or none above higher elevations.

3. Turbulence inversion (Air drainage temperature inversion)

A turbulence inversion often forms when quiescent air overlies turbulent air. Within the turbulent layer, vertical mixing carries heat downward and cools the upper part of the layer. The unmixed air above is not cooled and eventually is warmer than the air below; an inversion then exists.

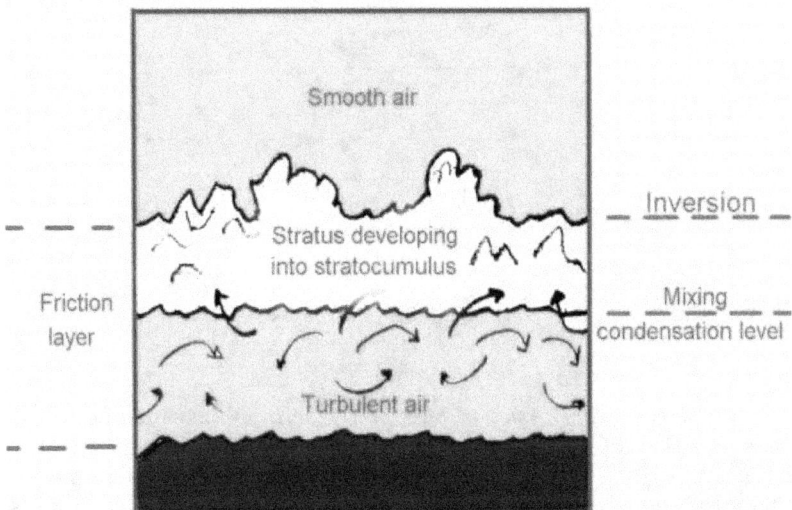

Fig.3.8: Turbulence inversion

4. Subsidence inversion (upper surface temperature inversion)

Caused by the horizontal movement of air occurs in several inversion. Such inversion is caused when warm air involves the area of cold air moves into the area of warm air because warm air being higher is pushed upward by relatively denser cold air. So inversion of temperature occurs.

If the air mass sinks low enough, the air at higher altitudes becomes warmer than at lower altitudes, producing a temperature inversion. Subsidence inversions are common over the northern continents in winter and over the subtropical oceans; these regions generally have subsiding air because they are located under large high-pressure centre.

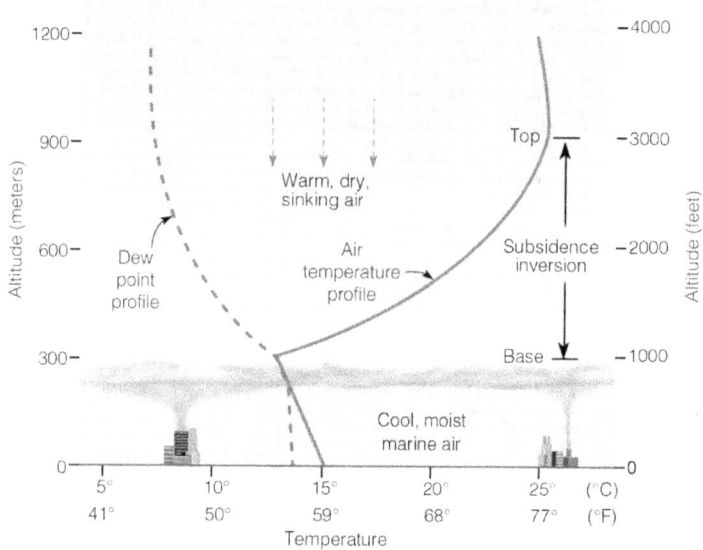

Fig.3.9: Subsidence inversion

5. Frontal inversion (Advection temperature inversion)
Frontal inversion it is also known as *cyclonic inversion*. It is formed when two constructing air masses coverage (warm and cold air). The warm air pushes up the cold and thus the warm air overlies cold. This type of inversion is common at the sub-polar low where warm westerlies and cold polar winds converge. This kind of inversion has considerable slope, whereas other inversions are nearly horizontal.

In addition, humidity may be high, and clouds may be present immediately above it. The ozone layer absorbs most of the ultraviolet radiation from the sun and thus the temperature of this layer becomes much higher than the air below it.

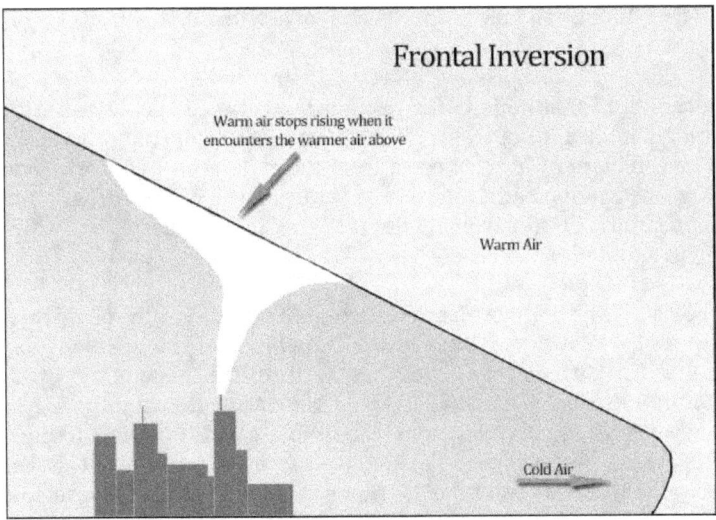

Fig.3.10: Frontal inversion

Air Temperature (Lapse Rate and Temperature Inversion)

Air temperature refers to the degree of hotness or coldness in the atmosphere. Air temperature is influenced by the amount of heat which is generated at a point in time. By heat, the energy in transferring influences the temperature of a matter.

Effects of Atmospheric Temperature

The atmospheric temperature (temperature of the air) influences atmospheric conditions in the sense that:

(a) It affects the amount of water vapor and thereby determining the moisture carrying capacity of air i.e. Warmer air is easily saturated hence carries more moisture as compared to cold air.

(b) It affects the rate of evapotranspiration and condensation, thus; governs the degree of atmospheric stability or instability.

(c) It influences the nature and type of clouds formed and consequently precipitation.

(d) Lead to the formation of cyclonic storms, fog, and smog.

57

(e) Air pollution can take place when there is temperature inversion.

Air Temperature versus Altitude

Air temperature vs. altitude is the relationship between "Cooling of Air and Adiabatic Change of Temperature Lapse Rate". The temperature is normally heated by condition of heat reflected from the earth. This is the reason as to why air nearest to the earth's surface is warmer than that at higher altitude. The temperature of atmosphere (in the atmosphere) decreases with the increase in altitude.

The process by which atmospheric temperature decrease with the increase in altitude it is known as *lapse rate*. Experimental observation of air temperature at different altitudes has verified the assumption that air temperature decrease as height increases. **Note that,** the atmospheric lapse rate is never constant, it varies from place to place and from time to time for practical purpose, it said to be at the average of $0.6°C/100m$ of ascent or $6°C/1000m$. Lapse rate is more in summer than in winter. Lapse rate is greater by the day than at night. It is also greater in elevated lands than at level of land (plain).

Types of Lapse Rate:

1. *Environmental Lapse Rate (ELR):* This refers to the situation whereby temperature decreases by the increase of altitude, i.e. $0.6°C$ decrease with increase of 100m. Environmental lapse rate is also called Normal Lapse Rate (N.L.R) or Constant Lapse Rate (C.L.R) or Vertical Temperature Gradient (V.T.G).

2. *Adiabatic Lapse Rate (A.L.R).* This referred to lapse rate when the temperature changes without addition or substitution of energy. In this, there is no gain or loss of temperature. Adiabatic mean without addition of heat energy. Adiabatic lapse rate have the following types:

(a) *Adiabatic cooling (wet/saturation adiabatic):* Saturated Adiabatic Lapse Rate (SALR) or Wet Adiabatic Lapse Rate (WALR) it takes place when there is cooling of pocked (parcel) of air without addition or substitution of energy. This change is $0.3°C$ to $0.9°C$ per 100m rise in altitude.

(b) *Adiabatic warning (Dry adiabatic):* This Dry Adiabatic Lapse Rate (DALR) is normally took place when pocked (parcel) of air warming without any addition or substitution energy. Takes place as temperature decrease by $1°C$ for every 100m rise in altitude.

Qn: *What do you understand by phenomenon of "temperature inversion" in meteorology? How does it affect weather and habitants of the place?*

CHAPTER FOUR

SOLAR RADIATION AND HEAT BALANCE

The sun is only important source of energy to the earth and its atmosphere. Millions of other stars radiate energy, but they are too far away to affect earth. Energy is also released from inside earth, primarily as radioactive minerals decay, but, only insignificant qualities. Tidal energy is also minor importance. Thus; the sun supplies essentially all the energy that supports life on earth and energize most of the atmospheric processes.

The sun is the star of average size and average temperature, but it is a proximity to earth gives it a far greater influence on our planet than that exerted by all other celestial bodies combined. The sun is a prodigious generator of energy. In a single second it produces more energy than the amount used by human kind since civilization began. The sun functions as an enormous thermonuclear reactor, producing energy by fusion, a process that burns only a very small portion of the sun's mass but proud an immense and continuous flow of radiant energy that is dispersed in all directions.

The radiant energy from the sun is in the form of electromagnetic waves. These are the waves that can transport energy without requiring a medium (the presence of matter) to pass through. They traverse the greater voids of space in unchanging from. The waves travel outward from the sun in straight lines at a speed of light – 300,000 Kilometers per Second. Electromagnetic waves are classified on the basis of wave length which can be thought of as a distance from the crest of one wave to the crest of the next.

Wavelength
Wavelength varies enormously, but for our purpose, the most important distinction is between *short wave* and *long wave* radiation. The dividing line between the two is a wave length of about 4 micrometers. Only a tiny fraction of the sun's radiant output is intercepted by earth. The waves travel through space without loss of energy, but since they are diverging from a spherical body, their intensity continuously diminishes with uncreated distance from the sun.

Intensity of waves

As a result of this intensity drop the distance separating earth from the sun, less than one two-billionth of total solar output reaches the outer limit of earth's atmosphere, having travelled 150,000,000 Kilometers in just over 8 minutes. Although it consists of only a minuscule portion of total solar output, in absolute terms the amount of solar energy earth receives is enormous; the amount received in 1 second is approximately equivalent to all the electric energy generated on earth in a week.

Basic Processes in Heating and Cooling the Atmosphere

Before looking at the events that occur as energy travels from the sun to the earth, let us look at the physical process involved in the movement of heat energy. There are **three** ways in which heat energy can move from one place to another by radiation, by conduction and by convections:

1. Radiation

Radiation is the process by which heat energy is emitted from a body. It involves the flow of radiant energy out of the body and through the air. All bodies radiate, but hotter bodies are more potent radiators than cooler ones. The hotter is the object, the more intense is its radiation and the shorter is the wavelength of that radiation.

Temperature, however, is not the only control of radiation effects. Objects at the same temperature may vary considerably in their radiating capability because the nature of the surface of the objects is an important determining factor.

2. Absorption

Heat energy striking an object can be absorbed by the object like water into a sponge, this process is called *absorption*. When insolation strikes an object and is absorbed, the temperature of the object increases. Different materials vary in their absorptive capabilities. The basic generalization is that a good radiator is also a good absorber and a poor radiator is a poor absorber.

Mineral materials (like rocks and soil) generally, are excellent absorbers. Snow and ice are poor absorbers. One important distinction concerns color; dark-colored surfaces are much more efficient absorbers than light-colored surfaces.

3. Reflection

Reflection is the ability of an object to reflect waves without altering either the object or the waves. Thus; in some cases insolation striking a surface in the atmosphere or on earth is bounced away, unchanged, in the general direction from which it come, much like a mirror reflection, where nothing is changed. In this context, reflection is the opposite of absorption.

If the wave is reflected, it cannot be absorbed. Hence, an object that is a good absorber is a poor reflector, and vice versa. A simple example is the existence of unmelted snow on a warm, sunny day. If it is melt, the snow must absorb heat energy from the sun. Although the air temperature may be well above freezing, the snow does not melt rapid because its white surface reflects away a large share of the solar energy that strikes it.

About *one third* of the total amount radiation from the sun is reflected back into space. This bounced radiation is called *albedo*. Albedo is a technical term of the reflectivity of the object. The higher is the albedo value, the more is radiation the object reflects. For example, dark soil reflects about 10% of radiation and absorbs the remaining 90% and a snow reflects around 90% of radiation and absorbs only 10% of radiation.

4. Scattering.

Particulate matter and gas molecule in the air sometimes reflect light waves and redirect them in a process known as scattering. This reflecting involves a change in the direction of the light wave but no change in wave length. Some of the waves are coming back into space and thus are lost to the earth, but most of them continue through the atmosphere in altered directions.

5. Transmission.

Transmission is the process whereby a wave passes completely through a medium as when light waves are transmitted. There is obviously considerable variability among mediums in their capacity to transmit rays. Earth materials for example, are very poor transmitters of insolation; sunlight is absorbed at the surface of rock or soil and does not penetrate at all. Water on the other hand, transmits sunlight well; even in very murky (dirty) water, light penetrates some distance below the surface, and in clear water; sunlight may illuminate to considerable depths.

In some cases, transmission depends on the wavelength of the rays. For example, glass has high transitivity for shortwave radiation, but not for long waves. Thus; heat builds up in a closed automobile left parked in the sun because shortwave insolation is transmitted through the window glass but the long wave that are reradiated from the interior of the car cannot escape in similar fashion.

In simplest terms, solar energy readily penetrates to earth's surface, but reradiated terrestrial energy is mostly "trapped" in the lower troposphere and much of it is reflected back toward the ground. This entrapment keeps earth's surface and lower troposphere at a higher temperature than would be in the case if there were no atmosphere. The circumstances just described are referred to as the greenhouse effect. Green house maintain heat in the same manner the glass roof transmitting shortwave solar energy in, but inhibiting the passage of long wave radiation out.

6. *Conduction.*

Another way in which heat energy can move from one place to another is conduction. The movement of heat energy from one molecule to another without changes in their relative position is called conduction. This process enables heat to be transferred from one part of a stationary body to another or from on object to second object when the two are in contact.

Conduction comes about through molecular collision and the heat passes from one place to another. The principle is that, when two molecules of unequal temperature are in contact with one another, heat passes from the warmer to the cooler until they attain the same temperature. The ability of different substances to conduct heat is quite variable. For example, most metals are excellent conductors, as can be demonstrated by pouring hot coffee into a metal cup and then touching your lips to the edge of the cup. The heat of the coffee is quickly conducted throughout the metal and burns the lips of drinker. On the other hand, hot coffee poured into a ceramic cup only very slowly heats the cup because such earthy materials are a poor conductor.

The earth's land surface, warm up rapidly the day because it is a good heat absorber and some of that warmth is transferred away from the surface by conduction. A small part is conducted deeper underground, but not much because earth materials are not good conductors. Most of this absorbed heat is transferred to the lowest portion of the atmosphere by conduction for the ground surface. Air, however, is poor conductor and so only the thin air layer touching the ground is heated very much. Moist air is a slightly more efficient conductor than dry air.

7. Convection.

In convection, heat is transferred from one point to another by moving liquid or gas. This method of heat transfer involves movement of the heated molecules from one place to another. Do not confuse this movement from one place to another with the conduction. In convection the molecules physically move away from the heat source; in conduction they don't.

Although the principal action in convection is vertical, there is some horizontal motion. When the convecting liquid or gas moves horizontally, the process is called *advection*. The heated air immediately above the fire is going upward because the heating has caused it to expand and therefore become less dense. The heated air rises-so the pressure is lower. Then the surrounding air moves to fill the empty space cooler air from above descends to replace that which has moved in, and a cellular circulation is established – up, out, down, an in.

A similar convective pattern frequently develops in the atmosphere. As far as our study of insolation is concerned the important points to remember about convection is that, it causes warm air to rise. Unequal heating may cause a parcel of surface air to become warmer than the surrounding air. The heated air expands and moves upward. The cooler surrounding air then moves in towards the heat source and air from above sinks down to replace that which has moved in. This establishing a convective system, the prominent elements of the system are an updraft of warm air and a down draft of cool air

8. Adiabatic Cooling and Warming

Whenever air ascends or descends its temperature changes. This invariable result of vertical movement is due to the variation in pressure. When air rises, it expands and less pressure is exerted on the surface. When air descends, it is compressed and more pressure is exerted on surface. The expansion that occurs in rising air is a cooling process even though no heat is taken away.

Spreading the molecule over a greater volume of space requires energy comes from the molecules. The loss of energy slows them down and decreases their frequency of collision. The result is a drop in temperature. This is adiabatic cooling, cooling by expansion in rising air. And vice versa – when air descends, it must become warmer.

The descent causes compression as the air comes under increasing pressure. The molecules draw closer together and collide more frequently. The result is a rise in temperature even though no heat is added from external sources. This is adiabatic warming—warming by compression in descending air.

9. Spatial and Seasonal Variations of Heating.

The world's weather and climate differences are fundamentally caused by the unequal heating of earth and its atmosphere. This unequal heating is the result of latitudinal and seasonal variations in how much energy is received by the earth.

Unequal Distribution of Heat

There are only basic reasons for the unequal heating of different latitudinal zones. See some of them:

(i) Angle of incidence.

The angle at which rays from the sun strike the earth's surface is called the angle of incidence. This angle varies with latitude. The larger is the angle, the more is concentrated energy and therefore, the more effective is the heating. Ray strikes the earth's surface directly, when the sun is directly overhead, and has an angle of incidence of 90^0(as above equator 20th of March and 21st of September).

Ray striking the surface at a slant has an angle of incidence smaller than 90 degrees, and for a ray striking earth at either pole, the angle of incidence is zero. Because the earth's surface it is curved and because the positional relationship between earth and the sun is always changing. If the angle of incidence is big, the energy is concentrated in a small area, and if this angle is small, it is meaning that, when ray strike earth's surface not directly but obliquely, the energy is spread out over a large portion of the earth's surface.

The more nearly perpendicular the ray is (in the words, the closer to 90^0 the incidence angle), the smaller is the surface are heated by a given amount of insolation and the more effective is the heating.

(ii) Day length.

The duration of sun light is another important factor in explaining latitudinal inequalities in heating. Longer days allow more insiolation to be received and thus; more heat to be absorbed. In tropical regions, this factor is relatively unimportant because the number of hour between sunrise and sunset does not vary significantly form one month to another. At the equator, of course, daylight and darkness are essentially equal in length (12 hours each) every day of the year. In middle and high latitudes, however, there are pounced seasonal variations in day length.

(iii)   *Atmosphere obstruction.*
The clouds, particulate matter, and gas molecules in the atmosphere either absorb, reflect or scatter insolation. The result is reduction in intensity of the energy received at the earth's surface. This weakening effect varies from time to time and from place to place, depending on two factors: The amount of atmosphere the radiation has to pass through and the transparency of the atmosphere.

The distance a ray of sunlight travels through atmosphere (commonly referred as 'path length') is determined by the angle of incidence. A large – angle ray (in other words, a nearly perpendicular ray) traverses a shorter course through the atmosphere than a small – angle one. A tangent ray (one having an incidence angle of zero) must pass through nearly 20 times as much atmosphere as a direct ray (one striking earth at 90 degree angle). Solar radiation is more depleted of energy in the high latitudes than in the low latitudes, thus; there are small losses of energy in the tropical atmosphere than in the polar atmosphere.

(iv)   *Latitudinal radiation balance.*
As the direct rays of the sun shift northward and southward across the equator during the course of the year, the belt of maximum solar energy swings through the tropical. Thus; in the low latitudes, to about 30 degrees, there is an energy surplus, with more incoming than outgoing radiation. In the latitudes, north and south of this parallel, there is an energy deficit, with more radiant loss than gain.

The surplus of energy in low latitude is directly related to the large angle of incidence, and the energy deficit in high latitudes is associated with small angles. There is balance between incoming and outgoing radiation for the earth or atmosphere complex as a whole; in other words, the net radiation balance for earth is zero. The mechanism for exchanging heat between the surplus and deficit regions involves the general circulation patterns of the atmosphere and oceans, which we will discuss letter.

(v)   *Land and water contrasts.*

The atmosphere is heated mainly by heat reradiated from earth rather than by heat from the sun thus; the heating of earth's surface is a primary control of the heating of the air above it. There is considerable variation in the absorbing and reflecting capabilities of the various kinds of surface found on the earth, for example soil, water, grass, cement, sand, roof tops. Their varying receptivity to insolation in turn causes differences in the temperature of the overlying air.

The most significant contrasts are those between land and water surfaces. The generalization is that land heats and cools faster and to a greater degree than water. So a land surface heats up more rapidly and reaches a higher temperature than comparable water surface subjects to the same insolation. These are several significant reasons for this difference:

a. *Water has a higher specific heat than land.* Specific heat is the amount of energy required to raise the temperature of 1gram of a substance by $1^{\circ}C$. The specific heat of water is about five times as great as that of land, which means that water can absorb much more solar energy without its temperature increasing.

b. *Sun rays penetrate water more deeply than they do land;* that is, water is a better transmitter than a land. Thus; in water the heat is diffused over a much greater volume of matter, and maximum temperatures remain considerably lower than they do on land, where the heat is concentrated and maximum temperatures can be much higher.

c. *Water is highly mobile, and ocean currents disperse the both broadly and deeply.* Land of course is mobile and so heat is dispersing only by conduction (and land is a very poor conductor).

d. *When land and water have the same temperature, a land surface cools more rapidly and to a lower temperature than a water surface.* During winter, the shallow heated layer of land radiates its heat away quickly. Water loses its heat more gradually because the heat has been stored deeply and is brought only slowly to the surface for radiation. As the surface water cools, it sinks and is replaced by warmer upwelling from below. The entire water body must be cooled before the surface temperatures decreases significantly.

The significance of these contrasts between land and water heating and cooling rates is that, both the hottest and coldest areas of earth are found in the interiors of continents, distant from the influence of oceans. In the study of the atmosphere probably no single geographic relationship is more important than the distinction between continental and maritime climates. A continental climate experiences greater seasonal extremes of temperature; hotter in summer, colder in water than maritime climate.

Mechanism of Heat Transfer

By definition, temperature is an expression of the degree of hotness or coldness of a substance. If there were not mechanisms for moving heat pole ward in both hemispheres, the tropics would become progressively warmer until the amount of heat energy absorbed equally the amount radiated from earth's surface and the high latitudes would become progressively colder. Such temperatures trends do not occur because there is a persisted shifting of warmth toward the high latitudes and consequent of the low latitudes.

This shifting is accomplished by circulation patterns in the atmosphere and in the oceans of these two mechanisms of global heat transfer, by far the more important is the general circulation of the atmosphere. Air moves in an almost infinite number of ways but there is abroad planetary circulation pattern that serves as a general framework for moving warm air pole ward and cool air equator ward.

The movement of the air (general circulation of the atmosphere) is caused mostly by uneven absorption of the heat at various latitudes, but also by the deflective force of earth's ration, which called the *Coriolis effects*. There is close relationship between the general circulation patterns of the atmosphere and oceans. Various kinds of oceans water movements are categorized as *currents* and it is air blowing over the surface of the water that is the principal force driving the major oceans currents.

In the other direction, the heat energy stored in the oceans has important effects on atmospheric circulation. There is a close relationship between the general circulation patterns of the atmosphere and oceans. All the oceans of the world are interconnected, because of the location of land masses and the pattern of atmospheric circulation; however, it is convenient to visualize five relatively separate ocean basins – North Pacific, South Pacific, North Atlantic, South Atlantic and South Indian. Within each of these basins, there is a similar pattern of surface current flow, based on a general similarity of prevailing wind patterns.

The movement of the currents, although impelled partially by the wind, is caused by the **Coriolis Effect**. This force dictates that the ocean currents are deflected to the right in the northern hemisphere and deflected to the right in the northern hemisphere and to the left is southern hemisphere. Each major current can be characterized as warm or cool relative to the surrounding water at the latitude:

1. California current (cool),
2. Equatorial current (warm),
3. West wind drift (cool),
4. Humboldt Current (cool),
5. Gulf Stream (warm),
6. Labrador Current (cool),
7. North Atlantic drift (warm),
8. Canary's current (cool),
9. Brazil current (warm),
10. Benguela current (cool),
11. West Austrian current (cool),
12. East Australia current (warm),
13. Kuroshio current (warm),
14. Oyashio current (cool).
15. North pacific drift (warm).

Vertical Temperature Patterns

Temperature in the troposphere is relatively predictable through the troposphere under normal condition; there is a general decrease in temperature with increasing altitude. However, there are many exceptions to this general statement. Indeed, the rate of vertical temperature decline can vary according to season, time of day, amount of cloud cover, and a host of other factors. In some cases, there is even an opposite trend, with the temperature increasing upward for a limited distance.

The rate at which temperature decreases with height is variable, particularly in the lowest few hundred feet of the troposphere, but the normal expectable rate is about 0.6°C per 100 meters. This is average **lapse rate**, normally vertical temperature gradient. The lapse rate tells us that it a thermometer measures a temperature 100 meter above a previous measurement, the reading will be, on average 0.6°C cooler. The second measurement is 100 meters below the first; the thermometer will register about 0.6°C warmer.

The most prominent exception to a normal lapse rate condition is a temperature inversion, a situation in which temperature in the troposphere increases with a height. The most readily recognizable inversions are those found at ground level. These are usually classified as **radiation inversions** because they result from rapid radiation cooling. They occur typically on a

69

long, cold winter night when a land surface (can efficient radiator) rapidly emits long-wave radiation into a clear, calm sky. The ground becomes soon colder than the adjacent air layer and now cools air by conduction. In a short time, the lowest 50-100m becomes colder than the air above. This type of inversion is more prevalent in high latitudes than elsewhere.

An inverted surface temperature gradient can also be the result of an **advection inversion** in which there is a horizontal inflow of cold air into an area. This condition commonly is produced by cool maritime air blowing into a coastal locally. Another type of surface inversion results when cooler air slides down a slope into a valley, thereby displacing slightly warmer air. This fairly common occurrence during winter in some mid latitude regions is called a **cold – air – drainage inversion.**

Global Temperature Patterns
Gross patterns of temperature are controlled largely by four factors:
- ☑ Latitude,
- ☑ Altitude,
- ☑ Land or water contrast and
- ☑ Ocean current.

Generally, the temperature decreases with altitude with some exceptions (inversion) and latitude (also with some exceptions, for example warm or cold oceanic current). Temperature distribution on the earth's surface may be represented by using isotherms, lines jointing points of equal temperature. General trends of the isotherms are west-east, roughly following the parallel of latitude.

If earth had a uniform surface and did not rotate, the isotherms probably would coincide exactly with parallels showing a progressive decrease of temperature pole ward from the equator. However earth does rotate and it has ocean waters that circulate and land varies in elevating. Consequently there is no precise temperature correlation with latitude and of course there are seasonal variations of the temperature. The isotherms follow the changing balance of insolation during the course of the year, moving northward from January to July and returning south ward from July to January.

Atmospheric Heat Budget
This refers to the metrological concept used to describe the balance achieved between the incoming and outgoing heat as no part on the earth's surface experience overheat or over cooling. Normally the tropical experience heat

70

surplus whiles the high latitude or polar and highland area experience heat deficit. Therefore, to avoid overheating on area, heating surplus and over cooling on area with heat deficient heat transfer takes place.

Types of heat transfer:
1. Horizontal (Lateral) heat transfer
2. Vertical heat transfer.

1. Horizontal (Lateral) Heat Transfer
Occurs through wind and ocean currents where there is transfer of heat from tropical to polar.

2. Vertical Heat Transfer.
Occurs through convectional currents, where heat is transferred from surface surplus heat to polar heat deficit.

CHAPTER FIVE

ATMOSPHERIC PRESSURE

Atmospheric pressure is also known as air pressure or atmospheric air pressure or barometric pressure. Atmospheric pressure is the force exerted by the gas molecules (included in the atmosphere) on some area of the earth's surface or on any other body including yours.

The pressure of the gas is proportional to its density and temperature. When air is heated it expands with decreases its density. Atmospheric pressure is the total weight of mass of column of air above, which average 1kg per square centimeter.

Atmospheric pressure is not constant through the atmosphere all the time i.e. some places experiences high pressure in sometimes while others experience low pressure. Atmospheric pressure also decrease with increase of altitude at the rate of 3:4 millibar (mb) per 600 feet, but this rate of decreasing is confined, but this rate of decreasing is confined to altitudes of a ten thousands meters (10,000m) only.

The instrument used to measure the atmospheric pressure called **Barometer**. And the lines joining the places of equal pressure at a sea level called **isobars**. The point of all this is that, atmospheric pressure is affected by both air density and air temperature and the relationship among the three variables intricate. It is important for us to be alert to these linkages, but it is difficult to predict how a change in one will. Weather stations normally record atmospheric pressures personal in units called **millibars**.

At the sea level the pressure exerted by the atmosphere is in average equal to 1000 millibars (it is slightly more than 1kg per square inch). Once pressure in millibars is plotted on a weather map, it is then possible to draw isolines of equal pressure called isobars. The pattern of the isobars reveals the horizontal distribution of pressure in the region under consideration. Prominent on such maps are roughly circular or oval areas characterized as being either **"high pressure"** or **"low pressure"**.

This highs and lows represented relative conditions pressure that is higher or lower than that of the surrounding areas. While highs and lows represent the pressure extremes in any region, less extreme pressure areas can be recognized on weather maps by the arrangement of the isobars. Isobars of low pressure and a trough of low pressure may separate two isobars of low pressure and a "trough" of low pressure may intervene between two isobars of high pressure.

On most maps of air pressure, actual pressure readings are adjusted to represent pressures at common elevations, usually sea level. This is done because pressure decreases rapidly with increasing altitude and consequently significant variations in pressure reading are likely at different weather stations, simply because of differences in elevation. This is the same with a temperature. The data for most maps displaying world temperatures patterns are modified by reducing the temperature to what it would be, if the station were at sea level.

As with other types of isolines, the relative closeness of isobars indicates the horizontal rate of pressure change or pressure gradient. The gradient can be thought of as representing the **"steepness"** of the pressure slope, a characteristics that has a direct influence on the speed of the wind.

Factors for Atmospheric Pressure Variation:

1. Temperature changes.
When or where temperature is high; air expands and rises creating a low pressure area where winds converge. Where temperature is low, air tend to contract and descend creating a high pressure areas where winds diverge. This is the reasons as to why in the poles there is high pressure. When air is heated becomes less dense and raises causing low atmospheric pressure and vice versa. When air sinks or descends its pressure increase, because it becomes compressed.

2. Altitude.
The atmospheric pressure it decreases with the increasing in altitude. This is due to the decrease in air density with the increase in altitudes. Due to this factor, the highest atmospheric pressure occurs at or near the earth's surface, particularly at the sea level where there is maximum compression of air caused by high gravitational forces (1013mb).

3. *Sun's Over Head.*
Variation in sun's overhead at tropics creates a considerable seasonal change of atmospheric or the surface.

4. Latitude.
The atmospheric pressure increase with the increase in latitude from the equator polar wards. This is the reasons as to why there is low pressure at the equator and high pressure polar ward.

5. Dynamic Factors.
These are the result of rotation of the earth and friction of winds across the earth's surface. These factors are responsible for creation of high pressure and low pressure areas, which are not related to maximum and minimum heating effects of the sun; for example: the occurrence of high pressure and low pressure areas in the temperate regions.

The Global Pressure Belts
The global pressure belts are also known as *'world patterns of atmospheric pressure distribution'* or *'horizontal distribution of air pressure'* and *'pressure belts'*. Atmospheric pressure is generally divided into two types:

(a) High pressure (high)
(b) Low pressure (low/depression).

There is no definite trend of distributions of pressure from equator towards the pole. If the air pressure would have been the function of air temperature above, there should   have been regular increase of pressure polar wards, and because temperature regularly decreases from equators towards the poles, but this is not the case.

The Major Global Pressure Belts
The major global belts of pressure include:

1. Equatorial low pressure belt (ELPB)
This is found along and near the equator (0^0-10^0C) North and South. It is also called *'equatorial trough'* and now referred as the *"Intertropical Convergence Zones"* (ITCZ). It is located on either sides of the geographical equator in a zone extending between 5^0 North and 5^0 South. But, this zone is not stationary base, there is seasonal shift of this belt extends up to 20^0 North in Africa.

The low pressure in this belt is due to heating effects of the sun. The equatorial pressure is thermally induced because the ground surface is intensity heated during the day and thus; covers most layers of air coming in contact with heated ground surface, also gets warmed. Thus; warmed air expands because is light and consequently is also called the belt of **doldrums.**

2. Subtropical High Pressure Belt.

Extend between the latitude 25^0- 30^0 in both hemispheres. It is important to note that, this high pressure belt has very high temperature than equatorial zone, but the zone is dynamical induced due to descending of upper air moving equator ward and causing the increases of air accumulation. The zone also called **horse latitude**. Therefore; there are two *subtropical high pressure belts* in each hemisphere.

3. Sub Polar Low Pressure Belt.

It is found between 60^0 – 65^0 latitudes in both the hemisphere since the zone experience low temperature. It is obvious that, thus; low pressure is dynamic induced. In fact the surface air spread outward from this zone due to the rotation of the earth and low pressure is called *Circum-Polar Low Pressure* Belt. Here we have two of them, one in each hemisphere. Centrifugal forces operating in this region create the low pressure belt. This region is marked by violent storms in winter.

4. Polar High Pressure Belt.

High pressure obtained at the poles throughout the year because of the presence of very low temperature (below freezing point) all the year round. It is found between the latitudes of 80^0 to 90^0 of both hemispheres.

Note: The planetary pressure system discussed, do not exist permanently throughout the earth as there is interruption of some factors which make them to change in some periods. The most on standing factor is the variation of sun's overhead which give to different temperature conditions and pressure systems.

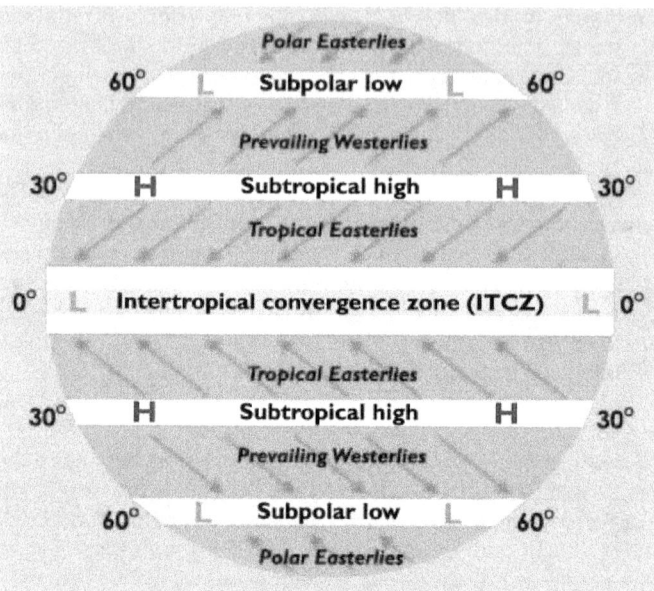

Fig.5.1: Global pressure distribution/belts

Qn. *Discuss for the planetary pressure system basing on their distribution globally.*

Temporary and Moving Pressure Disturbances

The atmosphere contains variation discontinuous pressure disturbances. These consist of cells of high or low pressure centers. The pressure cells are normally not constants permanent in the given area although they may stay over a particular area temporally but they are usually continuously moving. These pressure disturbances are caused by the *convergence* or *divergence* of air masses and they do affect the weather and or climatic conditions of the areas in which they occur. The pressure disturbances or cells are of two main types:

1. Cyclones
2. Anticyclones.

1. CYCLONES

These are also known as *depression* or *lows*. Cyclones are Centre of low pressure surrounded by closed **isobars** having increasing pressure outward and close air circulation from outside towards the actual low pressure in such a way air blows in-wards in anticlockwise in the northern hemisphere and clockwise in the southern hemisphere.

Simply, cyclones they have winds in the belt of westerly winds. They are pressures cells with low pressure centre which wind converge. The development of cyclones is caused by the meeting of cold air masses from Polar Regions with warm humid air masses from tropic as subtropical regions.

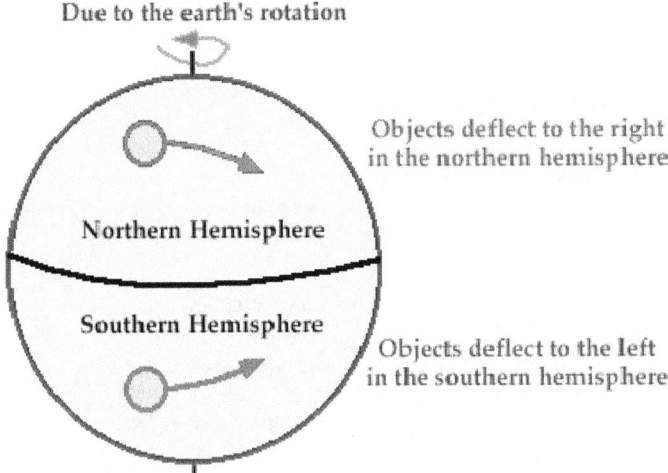

Fig. 5.2: Northern and Southern Cyclone

Stages of a Wave Cyclone

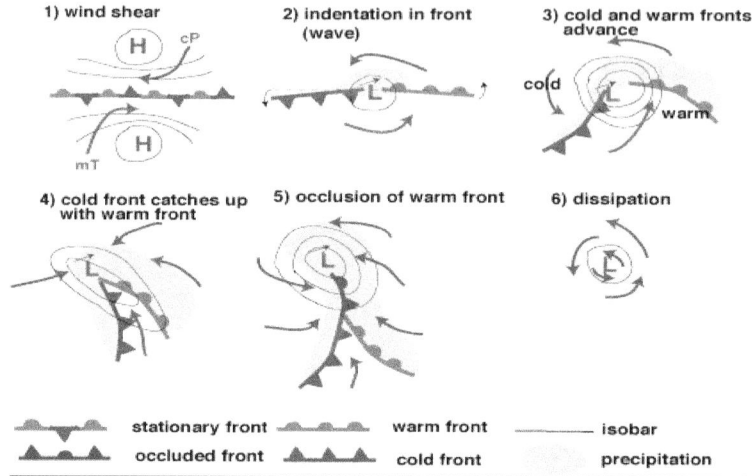

Fig.5.3: Stages of wave cyclones

Characteristics of Cyclones

Cyclones have the following general characteristics:

(a) They have isobars forming over or rough circle shapes whereby pressure is low at the centre and increase outward.

(b) They are rarely stationary and generally move in the westerly winds direction.

(c) They consist of swirling masses of air anticlockwise in the northern hemisphere and clockwise in the southern hemisphere to form westerly direction.

(d) Usually they bring prolonged rainfall and windily weather in the coasts.

Types of Cyclones

Cyclones are also formed as atmosphere disturbances. There are three different types of surface-based cyclone (Sub-Tropical cyclones) are included in temperate and tropical cyclones, hence makes the major three types of cyclones:

1. Sub-Tropical cyclones
2. Temperate cyclones (Extra-tropical cyclones)
3. Tropical cyclones.

1. Sub-Tropical Cyclones

A subtropical cyclone is a weather system that has some characteristics of a *Tropical* and an *Extratropical cyclone.* As early as the 1950s, meteorologists were unclear whether they should be characterized as tropical or extratropical cyclones. They were officially recognized by the National Hurricane Center in 1972. Subtropical cyclones began to receive names from the official tropical cyclone lists in the North Atlantic hurricane, South-west Indian Ocean and South Atlantic basins.

There are two definitions currently used for subtropical cyclones. Across the north Atlantic and southwest Indian Ocean, they require central convection fairly near the center and a warming core in the mid-levels of the troposphere. Across the eastern half of the northern Pacific, they require a mid-tropospheric cyclone to cut off from the main belt of the westerlies and only a weak surface circulation. Subtropical cyclones have broad wind patterns with maximum sustained winds located further from the center than typical tropical cyclones, and have no weather fronts linked into their center.

Since they form from initially extratropical cyclones which have colder temperatures aloft than normally found in the tropics, the sea surface temperatures required for their formation are lower than the tropical cyclone threshold by $3°C$ ($5°F$), lying around $23°C$ ($73°F$). This also means that subtropical cyclones are more likely to form outside the traditional bounds of the North Atlantic hurricane season. Subtropical cyclones are also observed to form in the South Atlantic; South Atlantic subtropical cyclones are observed in all months.

2. Temperate Cyclones.

Temperate cyclones also called *Extratropical cyclones, Mid-Latitude cyclones, Wave cyclones* or simply *depression.* The temperate cyclones are atmospheric disturbances having low pressure in the centre and increasing pressure outward. Temperate cyclones are mainly found alone at the polar fronts in the temperate regions where tropical warm air masses and polar cold air masses meet. They are produced in the middle latitude that characterized by converging and rising air, cloudiness and precipitation.

Temperate cyclones have no definite shape; they might be near circular or elliptical. They are normally originated in the region extending between $35°$ – $65°$ latitudes in both hemisphere due to the convergence of two contrasting air masses (cold, denser polar wind and warm, moist tropical air masses).

79

Temperate cyclones also greatly vary in size and extent, it may be pointed out that no two temperate cyclones are identical in terms of 150km to more than 3000Km. Wind blow from the periphery (outwards the centre). Because of **friction** and **coriolis force**, the northern hemisphere and clockwise in the southern hemisphere temperate cyclones moves.

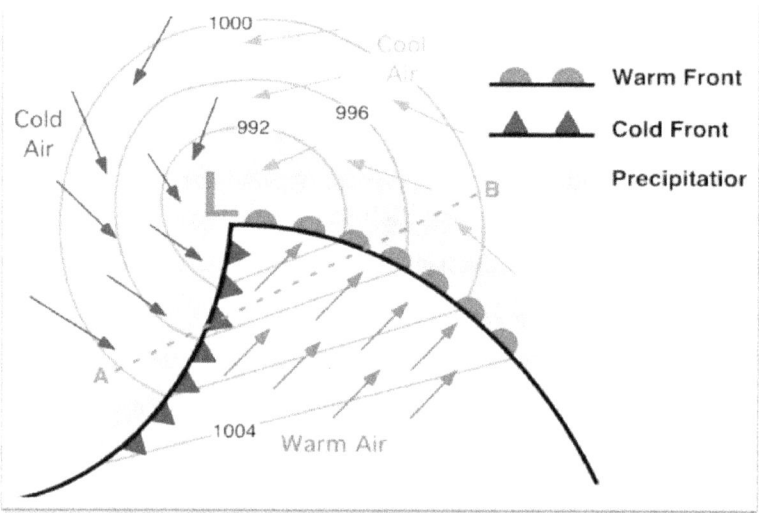

Fig.5.4: Temperate cyclone

Stages for Formation of Depression

a. *Incipient stage:* the wave has bulged leading to the formation of warm and cold fronts, and the warm sector.
b. *Open stage:* this is the mature stage. The wave bulged leading to the formation of warm and cold fronts, and the warm sector.
c. *Occlusion stage:* the warm front is occlude (or lifted off the ground) by cold front.
d. *Dissolving dissipation stage:* the depression become weaker and weaker and later dies away.

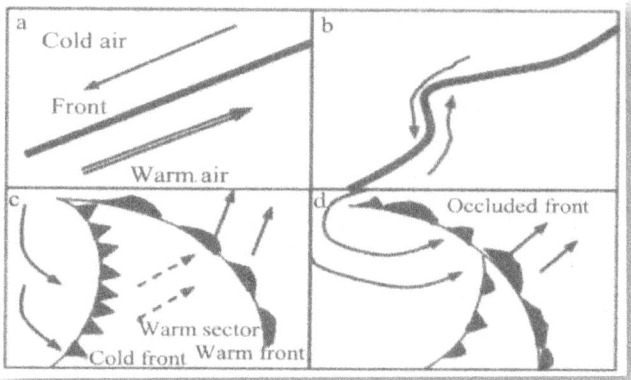

Fig.5.5: Stages for formation of depression

Types of Temperate cyclones

(a) Dynamic cyclones: These are real temperate cyclones because they are formed due to the convergence of cold air masses and moist maritime tropical air masses. Different fronts (e.g. warm front and cold front) and sectors (e.g. warm and cold sectors) are fully developed in dynamic cyclones.

(b) Thermal cyclones: Thermal cyclones are formed due to the development of low pressure centre on the continent in summer in the temperate regions and in the winter developed over warm sea water.

Weather Condition Associated With Temperate Cyclones.

The arrival of cyclones cause decreasing of air pressure, sky become over cast with dark, thick and clouds. The arrival of both warm and cold front, sky become over cast with thick cloud which yield heavy rainfall. The cold frontal rainfall is in the form of heavy down pour with clouds, thunder and lightning.

The centre of cyclones experience coldness and clear sky. Therefore, the weather conditions experienced when temperate depression occurs involves the following situation:

1. *Before the warm front passes:* here the wind blows south-west. The sky is almost clear and sometimes accompanied with high clouds i.e. cirrus

and cirrostratus. And after a moment, there can be stratocumulus and cumulus clouds accompanied with regular rains.

2. *When the warm front passes*: there is distinct rise in temperature and rapid increase in specific humidity. The rain stops and the wind changes from south-east to south-west.

3. *The warmer sector*: it has high temperature and high humidity with highly variable weather conditions, depending on the nature of the air masses and the season.

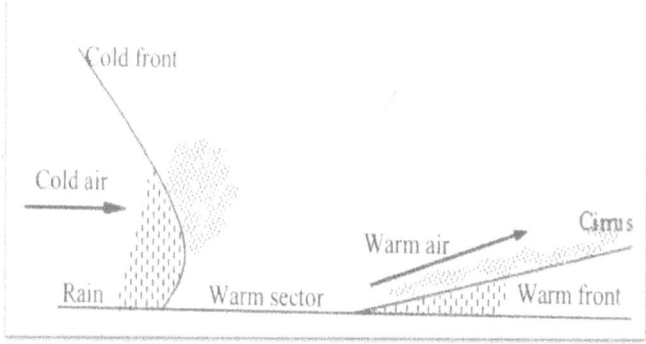

Fig. 5.6: Weather condition and temperate cyclone

3. TROPICAL CYCLONES.

These are cyclones, normally developed in the region lying between the tropics of Capricorn and cancer. They are intense and well developed low pressure centre, pressure cells into which violent winds blow (converge).

The Formation of Tropical Cyclone:

Information for the diagram below was retrieved from the Bureau of Meteorology (2015).

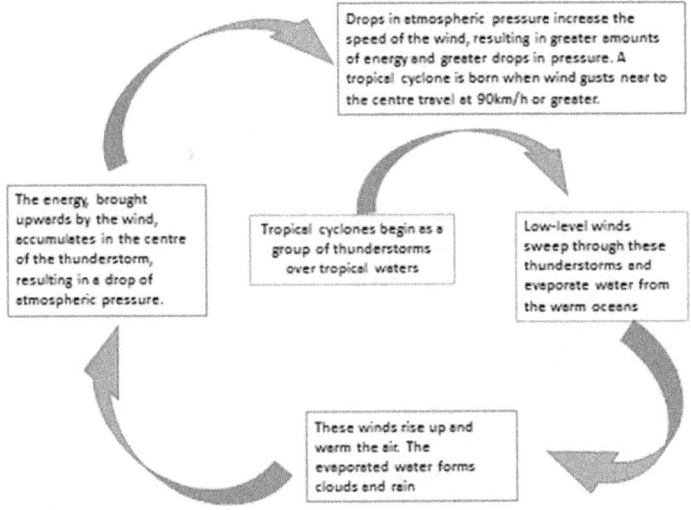

Fig.5.7: Formation of tropical cyclone

Characteristics of Tropical Cyclones

(i) Size of tropical cyclones varies occur, average their diameter range between 80km to 300km.

(ii) They advance with lying velocities, weak cyclones move at the speed of about 32km per hour, while hurricanes attain the velocity of 180km per hour.

(iii) Tropical cyclones become more vigorous and move with very high speed over the ocean than over the continents that is why tropical cyclones highly affects the coastal area like south and south east of U.S.A.

(iv) Tropical cyclones are not always and mobile, sometimes they become stationary over a particular place from several day and yield heavy rainfall causing flood and environmental disaster. The eye (centre) of cyclones is dry and rainfall is distributed in isobar.

The Structure of Tropical Cyclones

According to the Encyclopedia Britannica (2014), tropical cyclones have **three** distinct parts:

1. The Eye: The eye is the centre region of a cyclone; it is the calmest part of the storm unlike its surrounding regions. It contains clear skies, light winds and warm temperatures. It may be believed that the calmness of the eye is due to the fact that the cyclone is over. The eyewall and the surrounding rain bands are still due to come. The eye of a cyclone usually has a diameter of roughly 40km; however they can vary between 10km and 100km.

2. The Eyewall: The eyewall is the region of a cyclone that surrounds the eye. It is the most destructive part of the storm as heavy rainfall, extreme winds and very dense convective clouds driven from the eye create intense conditions for any type of environment.

3. Rain Bands: The spiral bands of clouds and storms known as 'rain bands' emerge from the eyewall of cyclones resulting in heavy surges of wind and rain. Cyclonic rain bands arrive in surges; there are often short moments of serenity, where no wind or rain can be found.

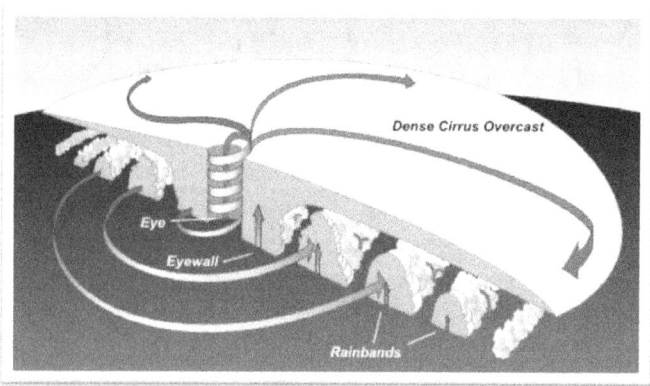

Fig.5.8: The structure of tropical cyclone

Different Categories of Tropical Cyclones

The intensity of a tropical cyclone is defined by **five** different categories; the higher the category, the greater the severity of the cyclone. The following information has been retrieved from the Bureau of Meteorology (2014); it clarifies the severity and potential damage that different categorized cyclones have upon the environment:

Category 1 Tropical Cyclone involves wind gusts up to 125km/h; they can cause damage to trees and farmland.

Category 2 Tropical Cyclone involves wind gusts between 125km/h and 164 km/h; they are classified as being 'destructive', causing potential house damage, and substantially affecting trees and farmland.

Category 3 Severe Tropical Cyclone involves wind gusts between 165km/h and 224km/h; they are classified as being 'very destructive', and can cause power failures and structural damage to houses.

Category 4 Severe Tropical Cyclone involves wind gusts between 225km/h and 279km/h; they can cause substantial damage to houses, and can cause widespread power failures.

Category 5 Severe Tropical Cyclone involves any wind gusts above 280km/h; they are classified as being 'extremely dangerous' and can cause total destruction upon anything in its path.

Difference between Tropical and Extra-tropical Cyclones
The following are some of the difference between Tropical and Extra Tropical Cyclones:

Tropical Cyclones	Extra-tropical Cyclones
Wind velocity is very high and more destructive	Low wind velocity and less destructive
Originate only on sea and dissipates on reaching land	Affect much larger area and can originate on land as well as sea

Table 5.1: Difference between tropical and extra-tropical cyclones

Weather and tropical cyclones association:
1. Before the tropical cyclones arrive, the air becomes very still and temperature and humidity are high.

2. As front of vortex arrives, the gusty winds develop and thick clouds appear.

3. When the vortex arrives, they become violent (upwards surges) and they often reach a speed of 24km and more per hour. Here dense clouds and torrential rain reduce visibility to a few meters.

4. The arrival of the rear of the vortex brings in violet winds, dense clouds and heavy rainfall. Here the wind now blows from direction opposite to that of the front of the vortex.

5. Calm conditions return when the eye of the cyclone arrives.

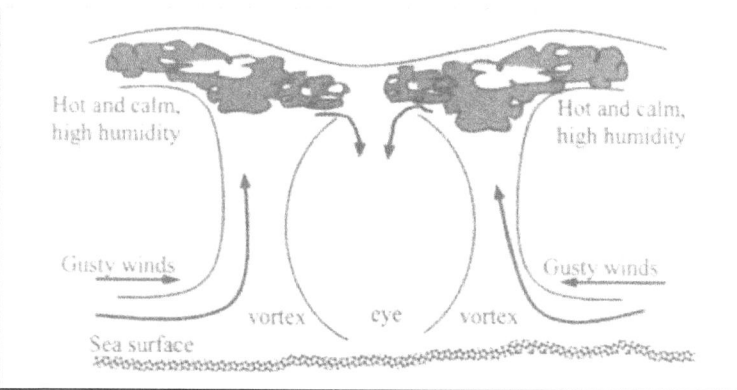

Fig.5.9: Weather and tropical

Types of Tropical Cyclones

Hurricanes and **typhoons** are the same storm types as "tropical cyclones" (the local name for storms which originate in the Caribbean and China Sea region respectively). Tropical cyclone is a non-frontal storm system that is characterized by a low pressure center, spiral rain bands and strong winds. A **cyclone** is an area of low pressure with winds blowing counter-clockwise around it in the Northern hemisphere.

Tropical cyclones are given different names to show how fast their winds are: **Tropical Disturbance** (winds are weak and unorganized), **Tropical Depression** (winds are less than 39 mph), **Tropical Storm** (winds are 39 to 74 mph) and **Hurricane** (winds are greater than 74 mph).

Also, **Meteorologists *see wind speed as one indicator as how much damage a hurricane can do. Knowing what may be damaged lets officials know what areas they should evacuate.*** The following are the groups and types of tropical cyclones:

1. Tornadoes
2. Thunder storms.
3. Tropical depression
4. Tropical storms
5. Hurricanes or Typhoon.

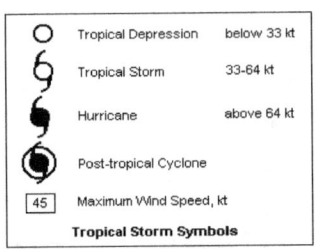

1. Tornadoes

Tornadoes are dark *funnel* shaped storms which are smallest but moist violent disastrous of all storms. They are very dark because of dominance of dust, sand, debris and condensed moisture. In other way, tornadoes also can be defined as *smallest intensive storm or vibration that characterized by localized by low pressure system that whirls both on the land and sea and associated by heavy rainfall and thunderstorms.*

Tornadoes they spiraling at a tremendous speed of about 800km/h with dark funnel cloud having 70 meters up to 450 meters diameter and are associated with cold front. Tornadoes normally heats along the latitudes 10^0 to 20^0 north and south of the equator.

The average life span of tornadoes is in minutes and it can cause a lot of damage. They are not so much common in many countries, but their effects concentrates in small areas, particularly in spring months. Tornadoes are common in Southern and Eastern U.S.A in the state like Florida, Mississippi, North and South Carolina, Georgia, Alabama, Texas, Tennessee and Kentucky.

Tornadoes in the mid of western state of the USA, they are commonly known as *Twisters.* Tornadoes can uproot trees, break branches, destruct buildings, other human structure and human deaths. Example on an average, the annual loss caused by tornadoes in the U.S.A damage to property worth 100,000,000 us dollars and 150 human deaths.

Fig.5.10: Tornado

Characteristics of Tornadoes:

(a) Tornadoes are associated with heavy rain, hails and thunderstorms

(b) They are accompanied with cumulonimbus clouds which are funnel like in shape

(c) They are very small and most destructive of all storms but in a localized extent.

(d) They are experienced in the higher latitudes, both over the land and the ocean.

(e) Winds in tornadoes circulate anticlockwise in the Northern hemisphere and clockwise in Southern hemisphere, and attain speed of 500 mile (800 km) per hour.

(f) Normally they occur in the afternoon during summer and spring.

2. Thunderstorms (Thunderstorms and Lightning).

Thunderstorms are also known as *electrical storms*, *lightning-storms* or thundershowers. Thunderstorms are local storms characterized by cloud thunder and lightning. These occur when masses of warm moist air along the surface are forced to rise rapidly upwards into cold dries layer of air.

Thunderstorms normally associated with cumulonimbus clouds which yield very heavy down pour in very short duration. They occur during the period of rise, electrical charges builds in the clouds. During the time of air upliftment of electric charges builds in clouds, both of lightening that caused by presence of positive and negative charges.

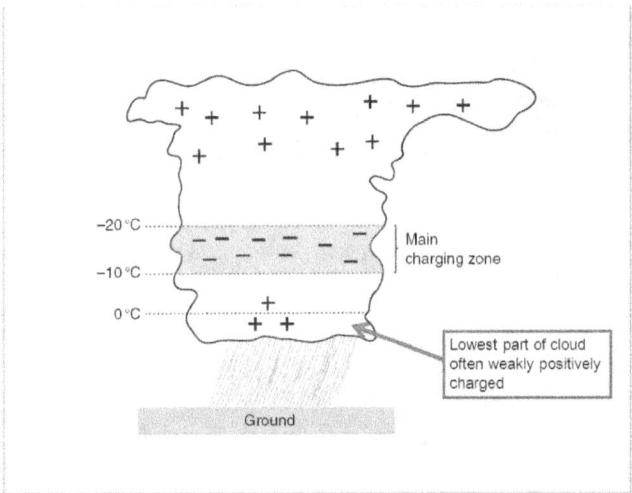

Fig.5.11: Formation of thunderstorm and lightning

Thunderstorms and lighting are formed when the great **hail** tends to cause condensation by convection; hence thunderstorm is caused by the energy released during condensation and electrical discharge that generate intensive heat. As a rainfall, positive charges of electricity is produced on **top** of the cloud and negative at the **bottom** when this happen lighting and flashes occurs by passing between the top and bottom, and between the bottom of the clouds, positive charges cause the thunderstorms.

The bolts of lightning leap from clouds and from the earth. A single belt of lightening may discharge million volts and is attracted to the tall objects. Therefore, atmospheric instability, abundant supply of warm and moist and thick clouds is important factors for occurrences of thunder storms.

Fig.5.12: Lightening in the sky after thunderstorm

Characteristics of thunderstorms:

(a) They last for a short duration, hardly two hours

(b) They are associated with heavy precipitation or hail

(c) They consist of down and updraft of air with electric charges and thunders.

(d) They are usually destructive in nature as they can destroy properties and kill people and animals

(e) They often built to great heights and more pronounced in terms of height in the tropical areas

Condition for formation of thunderstorms:

(a) There should be prevalence of atmospheric instability such that air updraft can set off.

(b) There should be availability of ample supply of atmospheric moisture for condensation to take place and maintain the storm.

(c) There should be some agent to start convection, such as uplift over a hill or mountain.

Stages in development of thunderstorms:

1. *Cumulus step:* in this stage, air rises within the cells to a higher level. In this stage, condensation occurs and rain or snow may results and when precipitation reaches the ground, results to the second step.

2. *Mature step:* there is exists of updraft and downdraft caused by precipitation when clouds extend vertically reaching the troposphere. The temperature in the downdraft is normally low and evaporation continues in the updraft. There are intense thunderstorms and heavy rains accompanied by strong winds. If hail is present, it falls at this stage.

3. *Dissipation step:* this begins when the updraft has disappeared. The downdraft dominates the entire cells and as the updraft ceases, the sources of condensing water is eliminated then the downdraft weakens. Cloud cover degenerate, into stratified clouds that spreading in the sky to complete dissipation

Lightning in a Thunderstorms

Lightening results from a change in the normal electrical field between the surface and the atmosphere. In a fair weather, the surface is negatively charged and the atmosphere is positively charged. Due to the intense friction of air with the cumulonimbus cloud, high charges are built up, with positive charges in the upper portion and negative charges in the lower portion. When the potential difference becomes more pronounced, discharges (lightening) occur from the cloud the ground or within the same cloud.

3. Hurricanes or Typhoons.

The extensive tropical cyclones surrounding (ed) by several close isobars are called *hurricanes* in the USA and *Typhoons* in China, they are also called *Willy willy* in Australia, *Cyclones* in Indian ocean, *baga* in Philippine and *Taifu* in Japan.

Hurricanes originated over the ocean between 5^0 - 20^0 latitudes in both hemispheres. They move with the average speed of more than 120km per hour. They have diameter which ranges between 160 and 640 kilometers. And the pressure at the centre ranges between 900 and 950mb which is the lowest pressure of a cyclones.

Hurricanes are associated with very heavy rainfall down pour. On the other hand there are no changes in which the direction in hurricane winds from outer margin toward centre, then arise upward.

Fig.5.13: Hurricane

In separation between hurricanes and typhoons can be clarifying as:

i.   Typhoons.

Typhoons occur mainly in between 6^0 – 20^0 north and south of the equator and are frequently from July to October. They have much greater pressure gradients and normally occupy a diameter of 80-320 kilometers. They are accompanied with:

- ☑ Violet winds of the speed of about 160km/hr.
- ☑ Torrential precipitation.
- ☑ Thunder storm – when it occurs, normally causes wide spread damage.

ii.   Hurricanes

These occur over the oceans between 5^0 – 20^0 north and south of the equator. They have more or less calm centers where pressure is the lowest but around the centre; wind speed exceeds 120km/hr. They are associated with:

92

- Dense dark clouds
- Violet stormy weather which last for several hours.

Hurricanes that strike land may cause violet winds, heavy rainfall and floods.

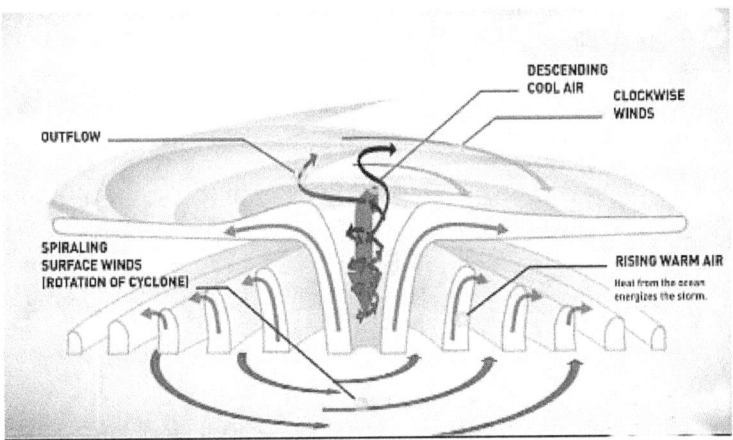

Fig.5.14: Structure of the Hurricane

4. Tropical Depressions

Tropical depressions are centre of low pressure surrounded by more than one closed isobars, and are very small in size wind velocity around low pressure centre ranges between 40-50 kilometers per hour. They usually develop in the vicinity of inter-tropical convergence zone.

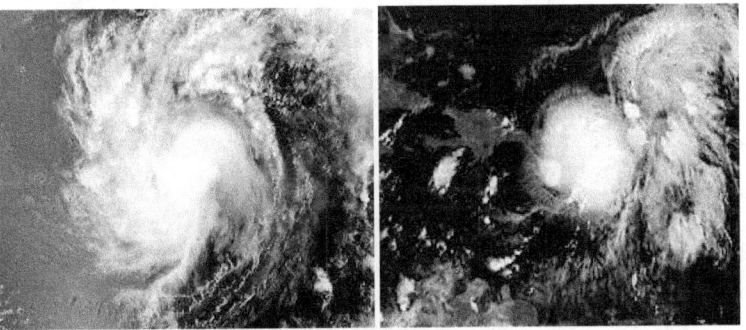

Fig.5.15: Tropical depression

93

Hurricane Stages

Tropical Wave	A low pressure trough moving generally westward with the trade winds.
Tropical Disturbance	An organized area of thunderstorms that usually forms in the tropics. Typically, they maintain their identity for 24 hours and are accompanied by heavy rains and gusty winds.
Tropical Cyclone	A generic term for any organized low pressure that develops over tropical and sometimes sub-tropical waters. Tropical depressions, tropical storms, and hurricanes are all example of tropical cyclones.
Tropical Depression	An organized area of low pressure in which sustained winds are 38 mph or less.
Tropical Storm	A tropical cyclone with maximum sustained wind speeds that range from 39 to 73 mph.
Hurricane	A tropical cyclone with sustained winds of at least 74 mph.

Table.5.2: Stages of Hurricane

5. Tropical Storms

By definition, tropical storms are tropical cyclones with maximum sustained winds of at least 34 knots (39 mph or 63 kph). Tropical storms are given official names once they reach these wind speeds. Beyond 64 knots (74 mph or 119 kph), **a tropical storm** is called a hurricane, typhoon, or cyclone based on the storm location.

A tropical cyclone has a defined cyclonic rotation and severe thunderstorms around a central low-pressure zone. The rotation of a tropical storm is more recognizable than for a tropical depression. Tropical storms can cause a lot of problems even without becoming a hurricane. However, most of the problems a tropical storm cause is stem from heavy rainfall.

A **tropical storm** is then upgraded into Category 1 **hurricane** status as maximum sustained winds increase to **between** 74 mph and 95 mph. The Saffir-Simpson **Hurricane** Scale is used to rate **hurricane** intensity in the Atlantic Basin as shown:

A Saffir-Simpson Hurricane Scale

Category	Winds (MPH)	Pressure (Millibars)	Pressure (Inches)	Storm Surge (Feet)	Damage
1	74-95	<980	<28.94	4'-5'	Minimal
2	96-110	979-965	28.91-28.50	6'-8'	Moderate
3	111-130	964-945	28.47-27.91	9'-12'	Extensive

94

| 4 | 131-155 | 944-920 | 27.88-27.17 | 13'-18' | Extreme |
| 5 | >155 | <920 | <27.17 | >18' | Catastrophic |

Table.5.3: Hurricane Scale according to Saffir-Simpson

Weather Conditions Associated With Tropical Cyclones.
The arrival of tropical cyclones at a particular place associated with:

(a) Increasing of air temperature.

(b) Increasing of wind velocity.

(c) Decreasing of air pressure.

(d) Emergence of high waves in the oceans.

(e) The clouds are thickened and become cumulonimbus which yields heavy rain associated with thunder and lightning.

(f) Visibility becomes zero because the sky is over cast with thick and dark thunder clouds.

(g) The arrival of the centre or the eye of cyclone normally is characterized by calm breezes, clear sky, rainless and fair weather.

Life Cycle of Cyclones:
1st **stage** - involves convergence of two air masses of contrasting physical prosperities and direction. This is called *initial stage.*

2nd **stage** - is called as *incipient stage* which the warm and cold air mass penetrates into the front of each other and thus waves like front is formed.

3rd **stage** – this is the *mature stage* when the cyclones are full developed and isobars become almost circular.

4th **stage** - warm sector is narrowed in extent due to the advancement of cold front comes to the front.

5th **stage** – start with occlusion of cyclones when the advancing front finally overtakes the warm front and occluded front is formed.

6th **stage** – is eliminated and ultimately a cyclone dies out.

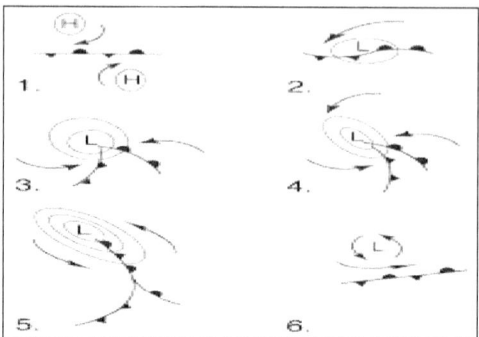

Fig.5.16: Stages/life cycle of cyclone

Apart from six stage of life cycle of cyclone, the following are four stages of cyclone as life cycle of cyclone according to the Norwegian cyclone model.

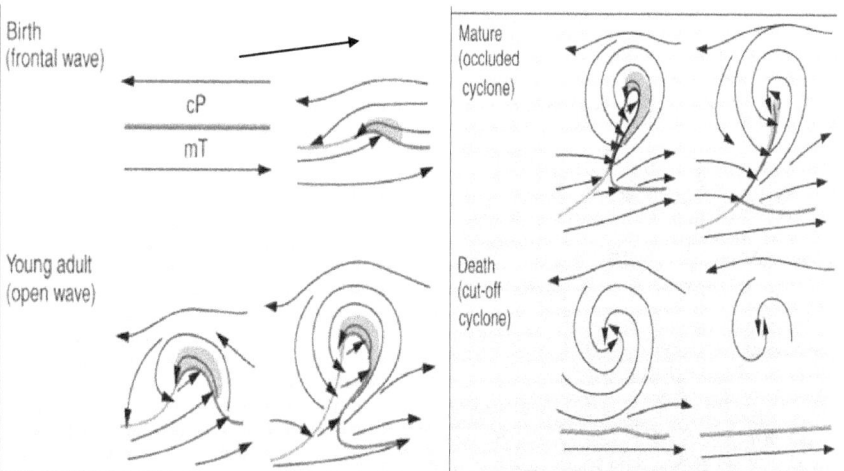

Fig.5.17: Four stages of cyclone life cycle based on Norwegian model

Environmental Impact of Tropical Cyclones

Tropical cyclones are very severe disastrous natural hazards which cause heavy loss of human lives and properties in terms of distribution of buildings, transport systems, water and power supply system destruction and communication system, destruction of agricultural vegetation and so on through damages caused by high velocity winds and floods.

The Difference between Hurricane and Middle latitude Cyclone

Tropical cyclones are violent atmospheric disturbances mostly formed and found on the western sides of the oceans in the doldrums between 6^0 - 20^0 North and South latitudes in both hemispheres. Tropical cyclones are known by various names in various places. For example, in West Indies, they are called *hurricanes*; in the Indian Ocean they are called *cyclones*, in China Sea they are known as *typhoons*, whereas in Philippines Islands they are known as *baguios*.

No.	Hurricane	Middle latitude cyclone
1	Are smaller but much more intense and destructive	Are large scale non-turbulent swirls or eddies
2	Formed in the tropics between 60 - 20 N and S, over the oceans on the western sides.	Formed in the latitudes between 45^0 - 60^0 N and S over the continents
3	Their central air pressure is much slower and pressure gradient much steeper	Has relatively gentler slope and the general movement of air is slow and continuous.
4	Has much higher wind velocity	Has lower wind velocity
5	Has no fronts	Has fronts, warm and cold
6	They are fewer in number e.g. only about 50 may be expected to develop each year in the entire northern hemisphere.	They are much more frequent e.g. 20 to 30 middle latitude cyclonic depressions may occur in one day during the winter months.
7	Has shorter lifecycle e.g. it may take only 6hrs to reach maturity.	Has longer lifecycle. It takes about 30 to 60hours to reach early maturity.
8	It has peculiar calm	It is a continuously developing disturbance.
9	Has a clear central area ranging between 16bto 80km wide from the ground upwards caused by descending currents called an "eye" of the storm.	Formed as successive sectors of air varying from each other in temperature conditions delineated by fronts.

Table.5.4: Difference between Hurricane and Middle Latitude Cyclone

2. ANTICYCLONES

Anticyclones are reverse of depression; air circulates away from the centre in a clockwise motion in the northern hemisphere and anticlockwise movement in the southern hemisphere. By a simple definition, an anticyclone is a pressure with high pressure centre. Their movements are common in the subtropical high pressure belt, but are practical absent in the equatorial region.

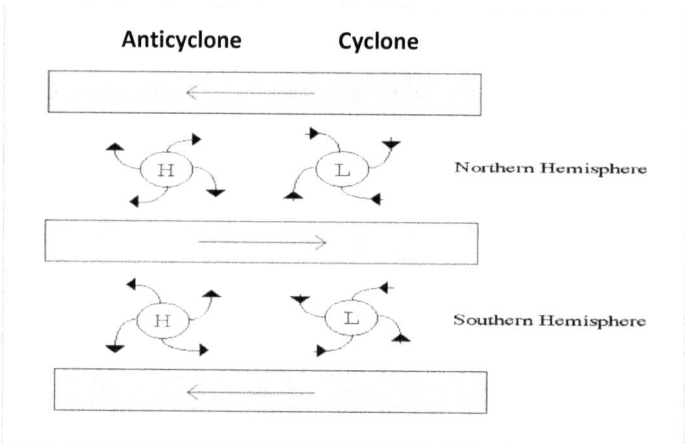

Fig.5.18: Anticyclones' direction in two hemispheres

They are associated with rainless, fair weather that is why anticyclones are called **weather-less** phenomena. This is because they diverge outward from the centre. In anticyclones, winds tend to blow outwards from the high pressure centre – clockwise in the northern hemisphere, and anti-clockwise in the southern hemisphere.

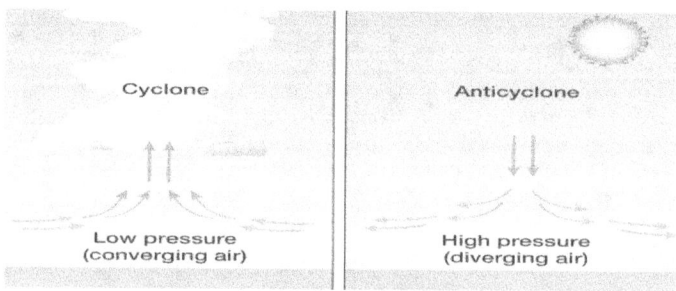

Fig.5.19: Anticyclone and cyclone in relation to high and low pressure

Characteristics of Anticyclones:

(1) They are large in size than tropical cyclones

98

(2) The average velocity of anticyclones is about 30-50 km/hr.

(3) Wind blow outward from the centre where there is low pressure area.

(4) They are not rain formation friendly due to air diverge from the center

3. OTHER KINDS OF STORMS

There other kinds of storms; the following are some of the other kinds of storms:

1. Line Squall

Squall is the word meaning to a sudden strong wind or short storm. Therefore, *Line squall* refers to the sudden violent winds that accompanied by precipitation advancing along a front that form a definite line.

They develops when the cool north-east winds undercut the tropical maritime air mass forcing it to rise and lead to very heavy rains accompanied by strong winds, thunderstorms and lightning. Line squall takes place at the beginning and at the end of the west season.

Line squalls are common and occurring in Nigeria, and the subtropical areas of the USA, east of the rock mountain in South America and in eastern India.

Characteristics of line squall:

a. They develop dramatically as a black line of cumulonimbus clouds that appears in the bright afternoon in the sky.

b. They are moved along a front from the east at a speed of 49 to 57km/h.

c. They consist of a number of thunderstorms and tend to move together in a line which can be hundreds of kilometers along; through they can just be 11 to 34km wide.

d. They are accompanied with intense heating, lighting and heavy rains, which can destroy properties like buildings and kill people and animals.

e. They sweep rapidly with violent winds and dusts, bending and thrashing trees and bushes and lifting some other heavier materials.

Stages in development of line squall:

1) *Step 1:* When easterly and westerly winds blow parallel along the inter-tropical fronts.

2) *Step 2:* When the eastern winds begin to thrust under the westerly winds, which are forced to rise steeply over the cold winds.

3) *Step 3:* When the active undercutting easterly winds forcing the westerly winds to rise steeply leading to very heavy rains.

2. Water spouts

Water spouts are storms that characterized by rapid whirling water drops sent out with great force caused by intense pressure system that is similar to a tornado that develops over the sea. Storms associated with water spouts are less powerful than tornadoes and are common in the subtropical waters of the Gulf of Mexico and off the south-east of the USA.

The rapid whirling water drops are derived both from condensation due to lowering of pressure in the centre of vortex; causes cooling and again from water picked up from the intensely disturbed water surface. From the low-lying base of the cumulonimbus clouds, a whirling cone of dark grey cloud projects downward gradually elongating until it touches the surface of the water.

CHAPTER SIX

WIND SYSTEM

Wind may be defined as the movement of air from high pressure belt to low atmospheric pressure in a virtually horizontal plane. There is a direct relationship between wind system and pressure system. Wind involves strength and specific directions.

Wind Direction and Strength Resulted for the Followings:
1. Pressure gradation and air circulation
It is the difference of pressure between any two places. Steep pressure gradient is represented by closely spaced isobars, while widely spaced isobars reveal low pressure gradient. There is a close relationship between gradient or barometric slope and air circulations. The winds normally move from high pressure to low pressure.

The direction of air movement should be perpendicular to the isobar by direction is deviated from expected direction due to the *Coriolis force* caused by the rotation of the earth. If the distance between high and low pressure zone is short, pressure gradient are steeper and wide velocity is greater.

2. Coriolis force (Deflection force)
This force proposed by famous scientist *Gaspard Gustave Coriolis*, that earlier was stated in term of *Ferrell's law*. A body moving on the surface of the earth it deflects to its own right in the northern hemisphere and it's left in the southern hemisphere as a result of earth rotation. This has affected on oceanic currents, tidal movement and winds. The force is proportioned to the speed of the moving object and it varies with latitude being zero at the equator and at a maximum at the poles.

When a balanced condition develops between the force exerted by the pressure gradient in one direction and the Coriolis force in the opposite direction a steady upper wind will blow. This is known as *Geostrophic Flow* or as *Geostrophic Wind* in a direction on parallel to the straight isobar.

3. Centrifugal Force

Also it is called *centrifugal acceleration* as the air flows around high and low pressure centers; it is influenced by centrifugal force. This acceleration is directed outward from both high and low pressure centers. Centrifugal acceleration is much more important for circulations, smaller than the multitude cyclone.

4. *The effect of friction (friction deceleration)*

Friction force not only accelerates the speed of wind but also deflects them. The friction is effective up to the height of a few thousands only. In one way or another, atmospheric motions of wind involve both horizontal and vertical displacement. Small scale vertical motions are normally referred to as **updraft** and **downdraft**. Large-scale vertical movements are called **ascents** and **descents** (or subsidence); the term wind is applied only to horizontal motions.

The insolation is the ultimate cause of wind, because winds originate from the same basic sequence of events. Unequal heating of different part of earth's surface cause temperature gradients that generate pressure gradients and these pressure gradients set air into motion. Wind are **"devices"** which even out the uneven distribution of pressure over earth.

Airs flow from areas of high pressure to areas of low pressure. If the earth did not rotate and if there were no such thing as friction, that is precisely what would happen – a direct movement of air from a high – Pressure region to a low – pressure region. However; rotation and friction both exist, and so this general statement is usually not complete accurate. The direction of wind movement is determined principally by the interaction of three factors; *Pressure gradient, the Coriolis Effect and friction.*

In the lower portion of the troposphere, a third force influences wind direction–the force of friction. The friction drag of earth's surface acts both to slow down wind movement and to modify its direction. Instead of blowing perpendicular to the isobars (in response to the pressure gradient) or parallel to them (in response to Coriolis effects), the wind takes an intermediate course between the two and crosses the isobars at some angle that is larger than $0°$ but less than $90°$. As a general rule, the frictional influence is greatest near the earth's surface and diminishes progressively upward.

The angle of wind flow across the isobars is greater at low altitudes and becomes smaller at increasing elevations. The effect of friction extends to only about 1500 meters above the ground. Higher than that, most winds follow a *geostrophic* course (parallel to the isobar). Distinct and predictable wind flow patterns develop around all high–pressure (Anticyclone) and low pressure (Cyclone) centers. Their patterns are determined by *pressure gradient, Coriolis effects and high - pressure cells and four with low pressure centre.*

Circulation Patterns
The circulation patterns are into two as namely below:
  (a) High pressure circulation patterns.
  (b) Low pressure circulation patterns

General Circulation of the Atmosphere
The earth's atmosphere is an extraordinary dynamic medium. It is constantly in motion. Some atmospheric motions are broad scale, and sweeping; others are minute and momentary. The general patterns of circulation involve major semi permanent conditions of both wind and pressure. This circulation is the principal mechanism for both longitudinal and latitudinal heat transfer and is exceeded only by the global pattern of insolation as a determinant of world climates.

If earth were a no rotating sphere of uniform surface we could expect a very simple circulation pattern. Insolation heating in the equatorial region would produce belt of low pressure around the world, and traditional cooling at the poles would develop a cap of high pressure in those areas. Air would rise at the equator and flow toward the poles, where it would subside into polar highs. Surface winds in the northern hemisphere would blow directly from the pole to the equator and in southern hemisphere in the same pattern, without any bending on the left or right.

The earth does have seven surface components, which are replicated north and south of the equator. From pole to equator, the names are as follows:
  1. Polar high
  2. Polar easterlies
  3. Sub-polar
  4. Westerlies
  5. Sub-tropical high
  6. Trade winds
  7. Inter tropical convergence zone

Atmospheric circulation is essentially a closed system, which neither a

103

beginning nor an end. In the sub-tropical latitudes there are four or five oceanic basins, which serve as the **"source"** of the major surface winds of the planet: *Hawaiian high, Azores high, south pacific high, and Indian high*. Each ocean basin has a large semi permanent high-pressure cells centered at about 30° of latitude called *Sub-Tropical Highs* (STHs).

These gigantic anticyclones, with an average diameter of about 3000 km are usually elongated **east-west** and tend to be centered in the eastern portions of basins. Their latitudinal positions vary from time to time, shifting a few degrees pole ward in summer and a few degrees equator ward in winter. From the global standpoint the sub-tropical highs represent intensified cells of high pressure in two ridges of latitudes, one in each hemisphere.

The high-Pressure ridges are significantly broken up over the continents, especially in summer when high land temperatures produce lower air pressure but the STHs normally persist over the ocean basins throughout the year because temperature and pressures they remain essentially constant. Within an STH, the weather is nearly always clear, warm and calm. These are characterized by warm, tropical sunshine and an absence of wind. Thus it comes as no surprise that these anticyclonic subsiding-air regions coincide with most of world's major deserts.

Modification of the General Circulation
There are modifiers of general circulation of winds as explained in the following:
(1) Seasonal variation in location
The seven surface components shift latitudinally with the hanging seasons. When sunlight is concentrated in the Northern hemisphere (North Hemisphere summer), all components are displaced northward. During the opposite season (Southern hemisphere summer), everything is shifted southward.

The displacement is greatest in the low latitudes and least in the Polar Regions. The ITCZ for example can be found as much as 25° north of the equator in July and 20° South's the equator in January. The pole highs experience little or no latitude displacement from season to season.

(2) Monsoons
By far the most significant disturbances of the pattern of general circulation are the development of monsoons in certain parts of the world, particularly southern and eastern Asia. The monsoon is a seasonal reversal of winds, a

general sea-to-land movement (called **onshore flow**) in summer, and general sea-to-land movement (called **offshore flow**) in winter.

Associated with the monsoon wind pattern is a distinctive seasonal precipitation regime–heavy summer rain derived from the moist maritime air of the onshore flow and a pronounced winter dry season on when continental air moving seaward dominates the circulation.

It would be convenient to explain monsoonal circulation on the basis of the unequal heating of continents and oceans. A strong thermal (in other words, heat-produced) low pressure generated over a continental land mass in summer would attract oceanic air onshore; similarly, a prominent thermal anticyclone in winter over a continent would produce an offshore circulation.

There are two major monsoonal systems (one in South Asia and the other in East Asia); two minor systems (in Australia and West Africa), and several other regions where monsoonal tendencies develop. The South Asia monsoon is characterized by a strong onshore flow in summer and a somewhat less pounced offshore flow in winter. In East Asia, the out blowing winter monsoon is stronger than in the blowing summer monsoon.

In one of the two minor systems, the northern quarter of the Australian continent experiences a distinct monsoonal circulation, with onshore flow from the north during the height of the Australian summer and dry, southerly, offshore flow during most of the rest of the year. The south facing coast of West Africa is dominated by the second minor circulation monsoonal circulation within about 650 kilometers of the coast.

Small Scales of Atmospheric Circulation
A Part from broad scale circulation of the atmosphere discussed earlier, there are many kinds of lesser winds, however, that are considerable significance to weather and climate at a more localized scale:

(1) Sea and land breezes
Common local wind systems along the tropical coastlines and to a lesser extend during the summer in multitude coastal areas is the cycle of **sea breezes during the day** and **land breezes at right**. A sea breeze blows from sea to land, and a land breeze blows from land to sea.

This is essentially a convectional circulation caused by the differential heating of land and water surface. The land warms rapidly during the day, heating the air above by **conduction** and **reradiating**. This heating causes the air to expand and rise, creating low pressure that attract surface breezes from over the adjacent water body; because the onshore flow is relatively cool and moist, it holds down day time temperatures in the coastal zone and provides moisture for afternoon showers.

Sea breezes are sometimes strong, but they rarely are influential for more than 15, to 30 kilometers in land. The reverse flow at night is normally considerably weaker than the day time wind. The land and the air above it cool more quickly than the adjacent water body, producing relatively higher pressure over land. This air flows offshore in a land breeze (see the fig 40).

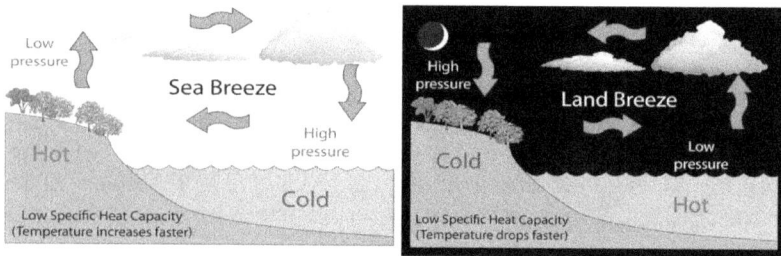

Fig.6.1 Sea and Land Breezes

(2) Valley and mountain Breezes

Another notable daily cycle air flow is characteristics of many hills and mountain areas. During the day, conduction and reradiating from the land surface cause air over near the mountain slopes to heat up more than air over the valley floor.

The heated air rises, creating a low-Pressure area, and then cooler air from the valley floor, flows upslope from the high-pressure area to the low-pressure area. This up slope flow is called a **valley breeze**. The rising air often causes clouds to form around the peaks and afternoon showers are common in the high country as a result. After dark, the pattern is reversed.

The mountain slopes lose heat rapidly through radiation which chills the adjacent air, causing it to slip down slope as a mountain breeze. Valley breezes are particularly prominent in summer when solar heating is most intense. **Mountain breezes** are often weakly developed in summer and are likely to be more prominent in winter. Indeed, a frequent winter phenomenon in area of even gentle slope is *air drainage*, which is simply the right time sliding of cold air down slope to collect in the lowest spots; this is a modified form of mountain breeze.

Relating to simple air drainage is the more general and more powerful spilling of air down slope in form of **Katabatic winds** (from the Greek word, means **wind descending**). These winds originate in cold upland areas and cascade toward lower elevation under the influence of gravity they are sometimes referred to as **gravity flow winds**. The air in them is dense and cold and although warmed adiabatically as it descends, it is usually colder than the air it displaces in its down slope flow.

Sometimes this wind will become channeled through a narrow valley where it may develop high speed and considerable destructive power. An infamous example of this phenomenon is the **mistral,** which sometimes surges down France's Rhone valley from the Alps to the Mediterranean Sea. Similar winds are called **bora** in the Adriatic region.

Another down slope wind is called **foehn** in the Alps, **halny** in Poland and **Chinook** in the Rocky Mountains (USA). It originates only when a steep pressure gradient develops with high pressure on the **windward side** of a mountain and a low-pressure through on the **leeward side**. The air movements down the pressure gradient, is the movement of air from the windward side to the leeward side.

The down flowing air on the leeward side is dry and relatively warm; it has lost its moisture through precipitation on the windward side and it is warm relative to the air on the windward side because it contains the heat received by the condensation of the vapour on the windward side of the slope. As the wind blows down the leeward slope, it is further warmed adiabatically, and so it arrives at the base if the range as warming, drying wind. It can produce a remarkable rise of temperature leeward of the mountains in just a few minutes. It causes a rapid melting of the snow (see the fig.41).

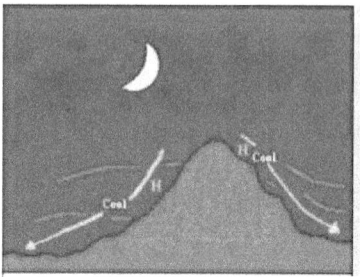 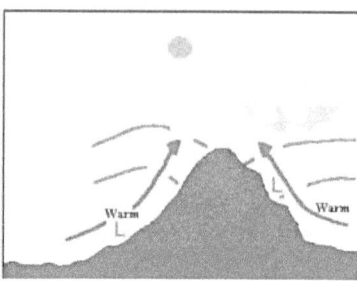

Mountain Breeze at Night   **Valley Breeze at Day**

Fig.6.2: Valley and mountain breezes

Classification (Types) Of Winds

Winds generally classified into three groups, which are:
(1) Permanent winds
(2) Seasonal winds and
(3) Local winds

1. Permanent Winds.

They are also called *planetary winds* or *prevailing winds* or *global winds*. These winds blow from high pressure belt to low pressure belt. The direction of these winds remains more or less the same, throughout the year that is why called permanent winds. Normally these winds blow in a definite direction crossing long distance and covering wide area. The nature of these wind are directly controlled by the ***global pressure systems***.

Also then are called planetary winds because they are related to the thermally and dynamically including pressure belt and rotation of the earth. Permanent winds subdivided into three types:
(a)   Trade winds or tropical easterlies winds.
(b)   Westerlies winds or Mid-latitude Westerlies winds
(c)   Polar (polar easterly) winds.

(a) *Trade Winds.*

These are winds blowing from the subtropical high pressure belt of both hemisphere towards the equatorial low or through, but as they are deflected by the Coriolis low or force they blow from north easterly direction on the northern hemisphere (north east trade winds). The name of trade winds come from the phrase **"to blow trade"** i.e. to blow steadily in constant direction. The name original hand nothing to do with trading although in sailing days these wind certainly furthered trade.

The trade winds known to its constancy of and direction and where north – east trade and south east trade converge is called Inter-tropical Convergent Zone (ITCZ) – they are deflected to the right in the north hemisphere and to the left in the southern hemisphere. There are two types of trade winds:

(i)   South east trade winds. They blow from southern sub-tropical high pressure belt equator wards.

(ii)   North east trade winds. These blow from the northern subtropical high pressure belt towards the equatorial low pressure belt. They blow from north-east direction.

(b) The Mid-latitude Westerlies

The permanent winds are blowing from the subtropical highs (30° – 35°) in both hemispheres to sub polar low (60° – 65°) in both hemispheres. The general direction of westerlies in South West (SW) to North East (NE) in the northern hemisphere, and North West (NW) to the South East (SE) on the south hemisphere or westerlies winds they blow from sub-tropical high pressure belts towards sub-polar or temperate low pressure belts.

Wresterlies which is warm and lighter converge with polar denser winds at sub-polar low and create what is so called **polar front**. Westerlies wind bring much precipitation in the western part of the continents (e.g. North – West Europe coasts) because they picks up much moisture while passing over ocean. Here there are both south westerlies (in the northern hemisphere) and north westerlies (in the southern hemisphere).

(c) Polar Winds/Polar Easterly Winds.

These are extremely cold winds which blow from the polar high pressure belt towards the sub-polar pressure belt. Cold air winds which blow from the polar highs to sub-polar low pressure cells. They are blowing north–easterly in the northern hemisphere. Here also there are two:

(i)   North polar easterly winds, which are found in the northern hemisphere.

(ii)   Southern polar easterly winds, found in southern hemisphere.

See figure that shows the general global wind system in relation to the pressure belt (the global winds and pressure belts).

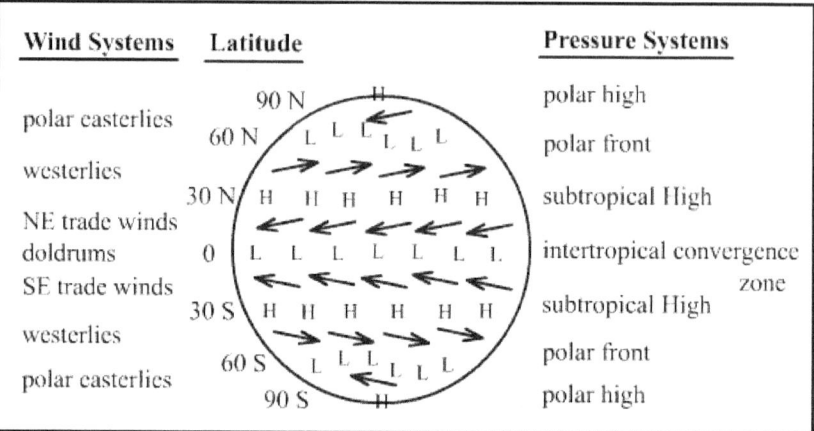

Fig.6.3: Global winds and pressure belts

2. Seasonal Winds.

These are winds with seasonal changes in their direction. The best example is monsoon (Manson) winds.

Monsoon winds

The word *"monsoon"* is derived from Arabic word *"Mausin"* meaning season. The word *mausin* was first used by Arabic navigators for the wind blowing seasonally over the sea between Arabic and Indian where they blow from North-East to South-West for **six months** during winter season and from South-West to North-East during summer season.

On this basis, the word monsoon was applied to all those winds of the globe, which direction changes from summer season to winter season and vice versa. The reversal of monsoon winds between two regions is caused by a reversal pressure system.

Origin of monsoon wind

During northern winters (winter solstice) when the sun become vertical overhead, the tropical of Capricorn in the southern hemisphere, high pressure pocket it developed over Asia, due to very low temperature. On the other hand, low pressure pocket developed in the southern Indian Ocean and Australia due to very high temperature.

Consequently, monsoon winds start blowing from Asia high pressure to the oceanic low pressure in Australia. The winds called *North East Monsoon*, because they are moving-north-easterlies from the high pressure pocked.

During northern summer, the direction of the monsoon wind will be reversed when the sun is over the tropical of cancer in the northern hemisphere. Because of high temperature, low pressure pockets developed over the Asia and high pressure developed over the Southern Indian Ocean and Australia due to low temperature. Consequently winds will blow from southern Indian Ocean high pressure to Asia which is experienced low. But the winds while crossing equator become south westerly (SW) due to Ferrell's law.

The winds pick up moisture while passing through the oceanic and yield heavy rainfall when obstructed effectively. The regions dominated by monsoon winds are called *"monsoon climatic regions"* which are more pronounced in Indian Sub-Continent, South East Asia, part of China and Japan.

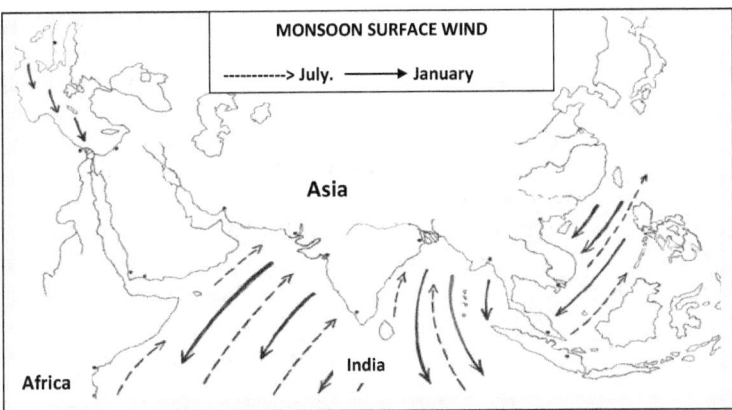

Fig.6.4: The Map showing monsoon winds direction

3. Local Winds.
By definition, local winds are the winds system which develop and are confined within different localities. Types of winds blowing in particular locality are called **local winds**. There are several types of local winds, these includes *land and sea breezes, mountain and valley breezes Chinook (Foehn), Hamattan, Sirocco, Mistral, Bora, Blizzard, Puogu etc.*

111

(1) *Land and sea breezes.*

Land and sea breezes have different characteristics of receiving solar radiation. Land had a tendency of getting heat first than the sea, but it lost heat energy very fast than the sea. So this variation produced winds that changes direction within 24 hours.

(a) Sea breezes.

During the day time land is heated more quickly than the sea. Consequently low pressure developed over the land due to the high temperature and high pressure will develop over the sea due to low temperature. Therefore, winds will blow from the sea to the land (high pressure to the low pressure). Furthermore, sea breezes become more active in each afternoon usually between 1 - 2 pm.

(b) Land breezes.

During the night, land lost heat energy in the form of terrestrial long wave radiation very quickly than the sea. As a result, land will experience low temperature with high pressure while sea it lost heat energy very slowly will experience high temperature with low pressure. Therefore, wind will moves from land to the sea low pressure.

(2) *Chinook and Foehn.*

They are notably as the warm and dry local winds blowing on the leeward sides of the mountain. They are called *Chinook* in USA and *Foehn* in Switzerland. The wind also called *descending wind or "snow eater"* and they are very common during winter and early spring along the eastern slopes of (leeward side) rocky mountains.

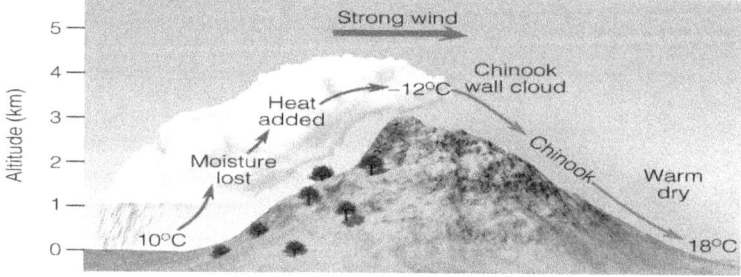

Fig.6.5: Chinook and Foehn

Foehn develops along the northern slope of the Alps Mountain and common during spring and autumn in Switzerland (see the fig. 6.5).

(3) *Harmattan.*

Harmattan is the warm and dry wind blowing from east-west across Sahara desert. While blowing over Sahara desert, these winds pick up more sands. Generally, Harmattan is very dust and stormy wind blowing with very high speed that could uproot along the western Africa. Similar warm, dry, very strong and dusty winds are called *"bruck fielder"* in Australia and *"blank roller"* in great plain of the U.S.A.

(4) *Sirocco.*

Sirocco is a warm, dry and dusty local winds blow in northern direction from Sahara desert and after crossing over the Mediterranean Sea reaches Italy, Spain, Portugal and other places alike. Sirocco while passing over the Mediterranean Sea picks up moisture and yield rainfall in the northern parts of Italy. This kind of rain is called *"blood rain"* because of all out red sands with falling rain. This is mainly because of mostly of the dust particles carried by sirocco from Sahara desert are red in color. Therefore sirocco called *"Khamsin"* in Egypt, *"Gibli"* in Libya, and *"Chili"* in Tunisia.

(5) *Mistral.*

These are cold wind which commonly blows in Spain and France from north-west to south-east direction (especially to Mediterranean). These stormy winds adversely affects are not flights and its arrival normally causes sudden drops in air temperature to below freezing point.

(6) *Bora*

Bora is an extremely cold and dry wind north easterly which blows along the shore of the Adriatic Sea. The Adriatic Sea is a part of the Mediterranean Sea positioned between the eastern coastline of Italy, and countries of the Balkan Peninsula, from Slovenia, south through Croatia, Montenegro, and to Albania. They are relatively (warm) dry over the Adriatic Sea.

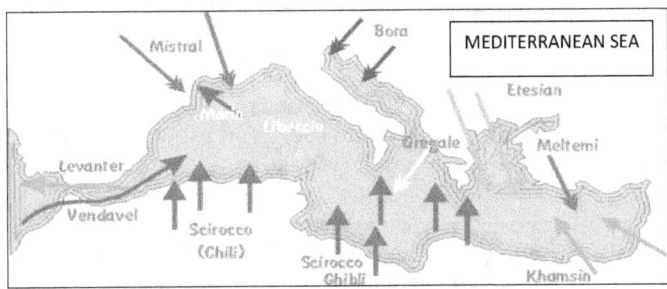

Fig.6.6: The map showing distribution of local winds around and near Mediterranean Sea

113

(7) Mountain and Valley Breezes.

Mountain breezes some time called *anabatic wind* blow down a valley during the night, while valley breezes blow up a valley during the day. *Katabatic* wind is the valley breezes. Gravitational force causes the heavy cool airs that accumulate over the snow in mountainous area to descending into lower valley location.

Consequently valley can become much colder than the slope area, the preferred sites for agriculture in mountain regions, because cold air from mountain breezes can cause freezing condition in the valley.

Mountain breezes usually occurs during the night in which air on the mountain is more cold and moving up the slopes in valley breezes caused by warm air moving up the slopes in mountainous regions. This occurs usually in day time. Example of mountain and valley breezes are canyons in southern California of mountain and valley breezes are canyons in southern California.

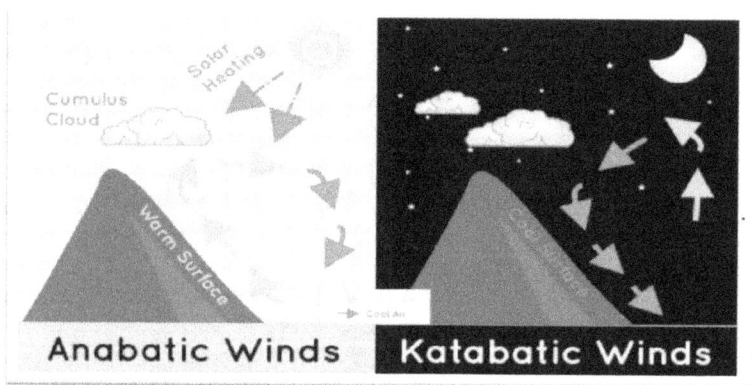

Fig.6.7: Anabatic and Katabatic winds

Some Other Minor Winds Related to Global Winds.

There are many minor winds related to the global winds, but some of them include doldrums winds, horse latitude winds and jet stream winds.

(a) Doldrums.

These winds are formed or found along or near the equator. They are sometimes known as *equatorial wind system*. These winds are light irregular in shape, calm and they are always rising. The rising of these winds is due to high temperature along this belt.

(b) Horse latitude winds.

These winds develop in the area where the trade winds and westerly (westeries) winds diverge. They are sometimes known as *tropical wind system*. They are light, irregular and calm.

(c) Jet stream.

These are the strongest belt of winds formed near the tropopause and they blow from west to east. They from where the warm air from tropics meets the cold air from poles at the higher troposphere. Jet streams follow the boundaries between hot and cold air. Since these hot and cold air boundaries are most pronounced in winter, jet streams are the strongest for both the northern and southern hemisphere winters. *Jet Streams are in Three Types*:

(a) *Polar Front Jet Stream (PFTS):* These occur in between 40^0 – 60^0 latitudes in both hemispheres. Then form a boundary between warm tropical and cold polar air masses. They also vary in extent, location and intensity and they are responsible for giving fine or wet weather on the earth's surface.

(b) *Sub-Tropical Jet Stream (STJS):* These occur in between 25^0 - 30^0 latitudes in both hemispheres. The STJS tend to meander less than the PFJS. They also have lower wind velocity but they are in the same direction as the P.F.J.S.

(c) *Easterly Equatorial Jet Stream (EEJS):* These are more or less seasonal jet stream. They are commonly associated with the summer monsoon of the Indian subcontinent.

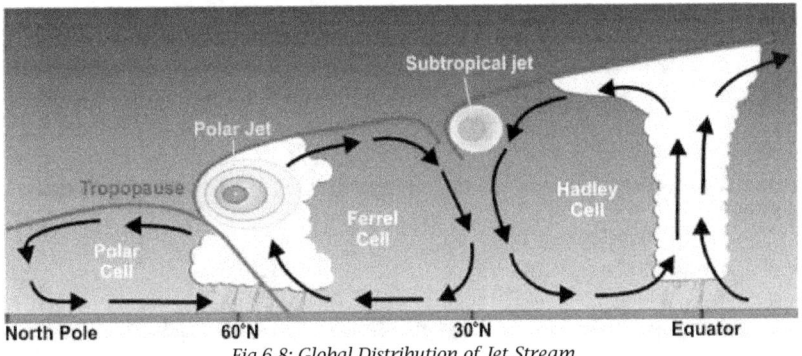

Fig.6.8: Global Distribution of Jet Stream

Factors Affecting the Strength and Direction of Winds

The following are some of the factors that affects strength and direction of wind:

1. Barometric pressure gradient.

This comes due to the pressure differences between high and low pressure areas. The pressure gradient creates natural flow of winds from high pressure area to low pressure area, i.e. the steeper the pressure gradient (indicated by the closer isobars) the strong the wind and vice versa.

2. Coriolis forces.

These are the forces created by the rotation of the earth. These are forces tend to be low or completely absent along the equator and they increase polar wards. These forces also are responsible for the direction of winds and other objects which are floating over the earth's surface i.e. they deflect winds to their right in the northern hemisphere and to their left in the southern hemisphere.

This is also known as *ferrelis law* of deflection, it states that *"any object that moves feely over the earth's surface will be deflected or turned away to the left in the southern hemisphere"*. Also coriolis forces are responsible for creation of low pressure belts in the temperate regions. Example sub polar (temperate) low pressure belt, these forces cause the existence of south westerly and north westerly winds.

3. Gravitational force.

Gravitational forces are the forces which pulls the objects (including wind) to the central earth's axis. These forces increase as one goes towards the equator. Since the central axis of the earth's pass through the equator the winds generally move equator wards.

4. Frictional force.

These are the force created by the dragging effects of the winds as they are moving over the surface. Note that; air (winds) moving over the surface has some of its mechanical energy transformed into other of energy that decreases its velocity and coriolis effects. At the surface, the wind direction crosses the isobars toward lower pressure. This occurs due to surface friction.

Friction slows the wind and this causes the Pressure Gradient Force and Coriolis force to not be equal since a slowing wind is less influenced by Coriolis. Since the Pressure Gradient Force becomes greater than the Coriolis and since air flows from high toward low pressure due to the Pressure

Gradient Force, the actual surface wind flows across the isobars toward lower pressure. The angle the wind crosses the isobars is more or less a 30 (10^0 over the ocean and 45^0 over the rough surface) degree angle.

This angle is less when friction is less but is more when friction is very high such as over a rough topographic terrain. Frictional forces are responsible for creation of low pressure cells in the temperate regions. When barometric pressure gradient, coriolis force and centrifugal forces as balanced in a state called *tropical balance*, a geostrophic wind will be created. A geostrophic wind is the one that blows parallel to the isobars. However it is very rare for such winds to occur.

CHAPTER SEVEN

HUMIDITY

Humidity (of air) refers to the amount of the water vapour present in the air at particular time and place. Water vapour simply is the gaseous form of water. Nearly half of the total atmosphere vapour is concentrated in low atmosphere up to the height of 200 meters. The atmospheric water vapour is dividing through evaporation of water from water bodies. Here water turned into vapour.

Evaporation and atmospheric vapour turned into liquid form by condensation from clouds and then water precipitated onto the earth from which a completely hydrological cycle. The presence of moisture in the atmosphere may be expressed as *absolutely humidity* and *relative humidity*.

(a) Absolute humidity.

Absolute humidity is also called vapour concentration (or vapour density). It is denoted by the actual quality of air or the total weight of water vapour content per volume of air at definite temperature.

(b) Relative humidity.

Relative humidity is defined as the ratio of the amount of water vapour actually presented in the air having definite volume and temperature (i.e. Absolute humidity) to the maximum amount of air can hold (i.e. Humidity capacity).

$$Relative\ Humidity = \frac{water\ vapour\ present}{water\ vapour\ required\ to\ saturate} \times 100$$

OR

$$Relative\ Humidity = \frac{Absolute\ humidity}{Humidity\ capacity} \times 100$$

When the humidity capacity and absolute humidity of air are the same, the air is said to be saturated and the relative humidity becomes 100%. In humidity, *mixing ratio* refers to the mass of water present in unit mass of dry air that expressed as grams per kilogram.

118

Capacity humidity refers to the ratio of mass of water vapour to that of the air containing it. The same as other elements of weather, also humidity can be affected or influenced by air temperature, precipitation, prevailing wind, presence of water bodies and presence of plant and vegetation cover.

$$Mixing\ ratio = water = \frac{density\ of\ water\ vapour}{density\ of\ dry\ air\ containing\ it}$$

$$Specific\ humidity = \frac{Mass\ of\ water\ vapour}{Mass\ of\ air}$$

$$Specific\ humidity = \frac{Density\ of\ water\ vapour\ present}{Density\ of\ dry\ air + Density\ of\ water\ vapour\ present}$$

Impact of Atmospheric Humidity

1. *Influence temperate regulation:* humidity tends to absorb heat energy and preserve it, such that the surface neither receives too much insolation nor does it excessively lose infrared energy into the atmosphere.

2. *Accelerates chemical process on surface and in the atmosphere:* for example decomposition of organic matter in the soil and rock weathering is high when there is high humidity.

3. *Condensation and precipitation:* presence of water vapor in the atmosphere accelerates condensation and formation of precipitation, since the water vapor tend to accumulate the atmospheric particles (aerosols) to form water droplets and later falls down as precipitation.

4. *Act as a control of evaporation:* low humidity in the sky, the rate of evaporation tends to be high and vice versa is true.

5. *Control of soil moisture:* the amount of soil moisture is determined by the humidity in the atmosphere. The areas with high humidity have moist soils, while areas with low humidity have fairly dry soils.

6. *Atmospheric purification:* when particles absorb water vapour and water droplets are formed which later fall onto the ground as rainfall

or any other form of precipitation leading to the purification of the atmosphere. Soil dusts are attached to surface where wind cannot easily blow the dust to great higher level in the sky.

Vapor Pressure and Saturation

Vapor pressure is the partial pressure that added in the atmosphere by water vapor. The limit of the vapor density of the atmosphere causes saturation in air. When the saturation point has been attained, might result to the condensation i.e. water change into liquid.

Influence of temperature on vapour pressure

Changes in temperature effect changes in the saturation vapour pressure. When temperature increases, also saturation vapour pressure increase; while, when the temperature decrease also the capacity of air to hold more water vapor also decrease. The critical point at which saturation point is reached is called **dew point**. Dew point refers to the temperature at which the quality of water vapor in the atmosphere is at its maximum possible (of the highest level of saturation). *Dew point is attained or reached through the following two processes:*

1. Through a decrease in temperature which leads to the reduction in the capacity of air to hold more moisture that later may lead to the formation of droplets.

2. Through the increase of water in the atmosphere, which leads to the formation of water droplets

Procedures in calculating dew points

1. Start by finding the difference (d) between the wet bulb and the dry bulb thermometer readings
2. Multiply the difference by the given multiplier (m)
3. Subtract the product multiplied from the dry bulb thermometer reading to get the dew point.

Example: Given the dry bulb (db) thermometer is $24^{\circ}C$ and the wet bulb (wb) thermometer is $18^{\circ}C$. What is the dew point if the multiplier is 2?

<u>Application</u>
$$db - wb = d$$
$$24^0C - 18^0C = 6^0C$$
$$d \times m = 6^0C \times 2^0C = 12^0C$$
$$= 24^0C - 12^0C = 12^0C$$
Therefore, dew point is 12°C at which water vapour will condense

Condensation and Sublimation

Condensation is the process through which atmospheric water vapour is converted into liquid as a result of cooling. Sublimation is the process in which water vapour changes directly into solid state without passing through liquid state.

Conditions for condensation

In order condensation to occur should involve the following conditions (condensation nuclei):

1. *There should be an atmospheric cooling*
2. *Existence of water vapour*
3. *Presence of microscopic particles in the atmosphere*

Forms of condensation:

1. *Dew:* drops of water that formed on the ground and other surface during night.
2. *Frost:* is the dews that become frozen
3. *Fog:* is the clouds of visible aggregates

The contrast between fog, mist and haze

1. *Fog* is the term used when the visibility is less than 1km. The term fog in Britain is used when the visibility is less than 200m.

2. *Mist* is the term used when visibility extend 1km to 2km.

3. *Haze* is the term used when visibility is limited between 1km to 2km as a result of dust or smoke

Ways in which air cools:

1. Direct radiation of heat energy from the surface leads to the cooling of the air, since heat energy is lost into the atmosphere

2. When horizontal air movement over the cold surface (advection).

3. Cooling can take place when warm air-mass meets with cold air mass.

4. Air tends to cool is by the air ascend through adiabatic cooling due to air mass expansion.

AIR MASS AND FRONTS:

(a) AIR MASS

According to R.G. Barry and R.J. Charley (1968), air mass is the large body of air whose physical properties especially temperature, moisture content and lapse-rate are more or less uniform horizontally for hundreds kilometers (100km). Also air mass can be defined as a large body or volume of air with uniform characteristics of temperature and humidity moving or covering a large area and moving along a considerable long distance.

Simply air mass can be defined as extensive body of air mass having similar characteristics i.e. designated as cold air mass when the temperature is lower than the surrounding surface. While an air mass is termed as *warm air mass*' is when the temperature is higher than the surrounding underlying surface.

Air masses are caused by the blow or are moved by planetary winds (the world wind system). Air mass originated when atmospheric condition remain stable and uniform over an extensive areas for fairly long period, so that the laying over that attains the temperature and moisture characteristics of ground surface. Also the surface origin the air masses should not experience the convergence of air rather there should be divergence of air.

Air masses which originated from oceans are called *Maritime air masses* (M), while these originated from land are called *Continental air masses* (C), air masses which originated from the tropics are called *Tropical air masses* (T), while those which originated from pole are called *Polar air masses (P).*

Effects of Air Masses on Weather

Air masses do control or influence the climate conditions in the areas they pass through or stay. Weather is highly governed either by the type of air masses in temporary occupation or when contrasting air masses converge. Example, when temperature forced to rise and ultimately will cause rainfall.

When two contrasting air masses converge, normally associate cyclonic storms, clouds and precipitation.

Modification of Air Masses

Since the world is prevailing in circulation air, masses tend to travel or migrate passing out of their source regions through areas with different surface. When this happens, the moving air masses characteristics might gradually be modified by the surface over which they pass. Also different air mass with different characteristics may meet and change characteristics of each other. Example, a cold dry air mass from the northern continents may move southwards over a tropical oceans. Here the air mass is readily warmed and its moisture contents air mass typical of new source region.

Convergence zones

Convergence zones are region where two air mass meet. There are two convergence zones:

(a) *That found along the equator where the north East trade winds and south east trade wind meet.* This convergence zone is called *Inter-Tropical Convergence* Zone (ITZ). This convergence zone is characterized by heavy rainfall or precipitation which is associated with thunder and lightning.

(b) *That found along the temperate low pressure belt (45⁰ - 60⁰) north and south where polar air masses converge with tropical air masses.*

Divergence zones

These are the areas where two air masses move away from one another (diverge). These zones are at 30^0 north and south at the poles. The divergence zones are characterized by high pressure, clear skies and very little rainfall.

Classification of Air Masses

There are two approaches which are normally used in classification of air masses. These included *geographical classification* and *thermodynamic classification.*

1. Geographical Classification

This classification based on the characteristics and features of the source (origin) of air masses:

(a) Tropical Continental Air Masses (TC)

The tropical continental air masses originated over subtropical high pressure with the continents and moving either equatorial of polar ward. They are warm and dry originated from the interior of the continents in the tropical regions and moved by planetary winds towards the equator or the sub polar (temperate climate). These air masses are responsible for the formation of hot desert such as Sahara, Atakama (Atacama), Arabian Desert.

(b) Tropical Maritime Air Masses (TM)
The tropical maritime air masses originated around subtropical high pressure but oceans. They are warm and moist air masses that originate from the tropical oceans and moved by planetary winds either towards the equator or the sub-polar temperature regions. Since they are moist and warm, they cause heavy rainfall on the coastal land into which they blow.

(c) Polar Continental Air Masses (PC)
The polar continental air masses originate over the continental interior; the northern tundra, lands of North America and Asia and the Green lands of ice caps. They are cold and dry, but when they spread out from the origin be modified. Example when polar continental air masses pass hot region will get warmed from and will become unstable. These polar continental air masses are moved by planetary winds towards the Sub-Polar Regions.

(d) Polar Maritime Air Masses (PM).
The polar maritime air masses are originated over the Northern Pacific and Northern Atlantic Ocean since they originate, polar maritime air masses are very cold and moist. They are also modified when spread out of the origin. Polar maritime air masses can yield heavy rainfall when they warmed from below and become unstable. They are cold and moist air masses that originate from the polar land mass and moved from planetary winds towards the sub-polar (temperate) regions.

2. Thermal Classification
Winds are classified according to latitude. Colder air masses are termed polar or arctic, while warmer air masses are deemed tropical. Continental and superior air masses are dry while maritime and monsoon air masses are moist. Weather fronts separate air masses with different density (temperature and/or moisture) characteristics.

(b) FRONTS.
Front is a line or zone where two contrasting air masses converge. Front also is defined as a line or zone of contact which is formed where two contrasting air masses with different characteristics meet. Sometimes fronts are referred to as *surface discontinuity*. When two air masses with different characteristics

meet they tend to mix instead they form a boundary (zone of discontinuity) known as front. The stormy weather is common in the fronts.

Classification of Fronts

Fronts are classified into four principles type on the basic of their characteristics:

1. Warm fronts (Cumulonimbus)

Occur when warm air and light air become active and aggressive and arise slowly above air cold and dense air. This formed particularly when warm air invades cold air zone. Warm fronts are associated with heavy clouds, heavy precipitation, and thunderstorms and lightening.

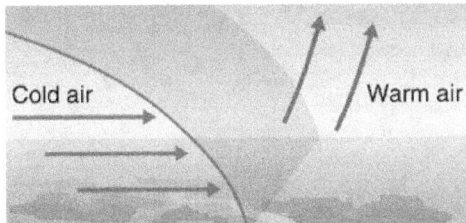

Fig.7.1: Warm front

2. Cold fronts (Nimbostratus)

Occurs when cold air become active and aggressive and invades the warm air territory and (being) air cold remains at the ground and forced the warm and lighter air to rise. The cold air mass forces the warm air mass to rise up rapidly. Cool temperature follows the passage of cold fronts. The uplifted warm air mass cools rapidly, condense rapidly there by form of heavy precipitation, thunderstorm and lightning.

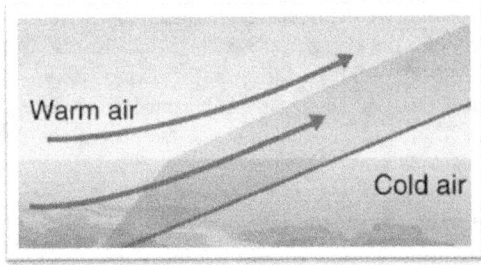

Fig.7.2: Cold fronts

3. Occluded front (Nimbostratus)

Occluded front is formed when cold front overtakes warm front and warm air completely displaced from the ground surface. The warm air mass hangs over the cold air mass. Occluded front is associated with heavy precipitation and thunderstorms (stormy weather) and high speed winds.

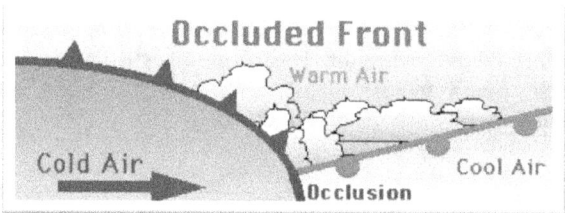

Fig.7.3: Occluded front

4. Stationary fronts.

It is formed when two contrasting air masses converge such a way that they become parallel to each other, there is no ascent. This is formed where a warm front, a cold front or an occluded front stays at a particular area for several days. This front is associated with sluggish (slow moving) wind and precipitation across the entire frontal region.

Stability and Instability of the Atmosphere

Different form of weather phenomena such as dew, fog, rainfall, frost, snowfall, hailstorm, sleet etc., depend on *stability* and *instability* of the atmosphere or the change in temperature and amount of water vapour in the atmosphere influences the stability of the atmosphere. This is manifested by the movements of parcels of air masses.

1. Atmospheric Stability

Atmospheric stability is the condition which the air in the atmosphere tends to rise or resist rising depending on the weather condition in the surrounding areas. Air is said to be stable when the rising parcels of air is colder or cools down more rapidly than the surroundings. When dry air which rising in the form of wind has lapse-rate greater than that of surrounding air and descents. This process causes stability of atmospheric circulation in which vertical movement of air is resisted.

Stable atmospheric conditions on the other are associated with fair weather conditions like cumulus clouds. In this, the environmental lapse-rate is less than the dry adiabatic lapse-rate. During stability the atmosphere is calm foggy and the air tend to move downwards. Stability is also called *stable equilibrium.* In this, there is no rainfall due to the absence of cloud formation. Temperature inversion is usually experienced, which act as a lid, blocking any rising air currents.

2. Atmospheric Instability (Atmospheric Disturbance)

By definition, atmospheric instability is the condition where the earth's atmosphere is generally unstable due to weather being high in degree of variability through distance and time. Instability takes place in the atmosphere when the parcels of air in the atmosphere are less dense than the surrounding air. The parcel of air tends to rise rapidly and it takes place more often in saturated air, because the saturated air tends to cool down slowly than the surrounding environment. The warmer saturated panels of air mass which is light manage to rise at a great height before cooling down and cause unstable condition in the atmosphere.

In unstable conditions heavy clouds are normally formed leading into formation of heavy rainfall, hails and storms. This disturbance is caused by horizontal movement of air masses, leads to the formation of storms. Instability is said to occur when ELR (environmental lapse rate) is greater than SALR (saturated adiabatic lapse rate). Unstable atmospheric condition is said to be *unstable equilibrium,* and at the point where warm air mass cools in ascending, the vertical movement ceases and it is said to be *neutral* or *indifferent equilibrium.* Both stability and instability are influenced by the movement pockets of air mass.

Conditional Instability: Conditional instability refers to the rate of cooling remains lower than its surroundings when warm air continue in ascending on its own after condensation. It is called that, because the instability is conditional upon the presence of sufficient water vapour. This occurs when dry air masses are forced to rise as wind up a mountain slope and keep on cooling at **DALR** (dry adiabatic lapse rate) until dew point is reached where condensation takes place.

After condensation, the airs acquires some moisture and hence continue to cool the SALR (in lower the surrounding) hence continues to ascent spontaneously (on its own) even if the initial force was mechanical. Important note is that, conditional instability does not necessarily take place after the air has been forced to ascend orographically. When air mass become *conditionally unstable* after being forced to rise over a relief barrier or over a cold air-mass at a font, it is named as a state of *potential instability.*

NOTE:
☑ The atmosphere is stable when ELR<DALR *or* DALR> ELR.

☑ The atmosphere is absolutely stable when ELR<SALR *or* SALR>ELR.

☑ The atmosphere is neutral equilibrium when ELR = DALR *or* DALR = ELR.

☑ The atmosphere is unstable when ELR>DALR or DALR<ELS.

☑ The atmosphere is conditionally unstable when ELR is between DALR and SALR.

Trial question: Discuss for the effects of atmospheric stability and instability.

Types of Atmospheric Disturbances
There are two main types of atmospheric disturbances as namely:
    (i) Polar disturbances
    (ii) Tropical disturbances.

1. Polar disturbances
They refer to the area of low pressure which is always circular form. They are developed in the cold areas that are 60^0 north and south of the equator. These caused by meeting between polar winds and subtropical weaterlies; on meeting start circulate anticlockwise at the northern hemisphere hence form a depression.

2. Tropical disturbance.
This takes place in the tropical climatic area. Tropical Disturbance is the birth of a hurricane, having only a slight circulation with no closed isobars around an area of low pressure. Tropical disturbances commonly exist in the **tropical** trade winds at any one time and are often accompanied by clouds and precipitation. Tropical disturbances look like an unorganized cluster of thunderstorms when viewed in satellite imagery. Depending on the atmospheric conditions around a tropical disturbance, it can either weaken or dissipate, or it can become more organized and strengthen into a tropical depression.

Air Mass Ascent

The panels of air masses are caused to rise by a number of factors:

1. Heating
2. Meeting mountain
3. Meeting two air masses.

1. Heating.

A panel of air mass can rise after being heated on warmed by conditions. In this case the heat energy reflected from the earth's surface warms the air which is above the earth's surface hence vertical – convectional currents occurs. This is very common in tropical areas where the overhead sun is common. This condition leads to the formation of clouds and convectional rainfall which is commonly occurs in the afternoon and it commonly accompanied with lightning and thunderstorms.

2. Meeting High Mountain.

The panel of air mass can rise after being forced mechanically upslope when wind blows against the mountain. The air mass forced to rise may cool down after having risen at the high altitude. Condensation and clouds may be formed leading to the formation of relief or orographic rainfall.

3. Meeting of Air Masses.

It is when warm and cold air masses meet the warm air mass which usually less dense is forced to rise above the cold air mass. On meeting, they form the front and warm air which is forced to rise up, may condense to form clouds and consequently frontal or cyclonic rainfall.

CHAPTER EIGHT

PRECIPITATION

Precipitation is any product of the condensation of atmospheric water vapor that falls under gravity. The main forms of precipitation include drizzle, rain, sleet, snow and hail. Precipitation occurs when a portion of the atmosphere becomes saturated with water vapor, so that the water condenses and "precipitates".

Thus, fog and mist are not precipitation but suspensions, because the water vapor does not condense sufficiently to precipitate. Two processes, possibly acting together, can lead to air becoming saturated: cooling the air or adding water vapor to the air. Precipitation forms as smaller droplets coalesce via collision with other rain drops or ice crystals within a cloud. Short, intense periods of rain in scattered locations are called "showers".

Precipitation is a major component of the water cycle, and is responsible for depositing the fresh water on the planet. Approximately 505,000 cubic kilometers (121,000 cu mi) of waterfalls as precipitation each year; 398,000 cubic kilometres (95,000 cu mi) of it is over the oceans and 107,000 cubic kilometres (26,000 cu mi) over land. Given the Earth's surface area, that means the globally averaged annual precipitation is 990 millimeters (39 in), but over land it is only 715 millimeters (28.1 in).

Climate Classification systems such as the Köppen climate classification system use average annual rainfall help to differentiate between differing climates regimes. Precipitation has positive impacts like: it encourage plant growth, facilitate temperature regulation, act as a cleaner of the atmosphere from pollution, influence water bodies' development and act as the foster for development. In other way, precipitation has also negative effects like cause for outbreak of waterborne diseases, occurrence of floods and soil erosion, and influence mass wasting to rocks.

Condensation Process
The transformation of a gaseous from water (i.e. water vapour) into solid from (ice) and liquid from (water) is called condensation. Air masses rise and when they become saturated, condensation will begin only when the air it is

upper saturated and this can be achieved when air reaches dew point (super cold).

If dew point is above freezing point, condensation will occur in the liquid form (e.g. dew, fog, rainfall etc). If dew point is below freezing point, condensation occurs in liquid, solid form (e.g. frost, ice, snow, hailstorm etc). In order for condensation to take place, there are several conditions that must be taken into consideration:

Firstly; there should be condensation nuclei around which water vapour will condense. These nuclei include particles of dust and smoke, salt from the ocean, pollen and meteoric particles.

Secondary; there should be water vapour brought in the atmosphere by means of evaporation.

Thirdly; there should be cooling effects to the extent of reaching the dew point.

1. FOG

Fog is a thin cloud consisting of microscopically small water droplets which are kept in suspension in the air near the surface and reduces the horizontal visibility (to greater than 1Km). The formation of fog, generally associated with temperature inversion and normally occur in morning hours, however sometimes can continue till noon.

In tropical and subtropical regions experience fog during winters but it occurs in all season in the middle latitudes. Generally, fog looks whitish in color, but over large cities and industrial area, it looks dirty, yellow or gray because of mixing of smoke, dusts and fly ash.

Classification of Fogs

There are several different **types of fog**, including the following:

1. *Radiation fog:* This is the fog that formed when warm and moist air lies over the cold ground surface. Due to this situation overlaying warm and moist air cools and thus dew point is reached, and followed by condensation process which turns water vapour into tiny water droplets and thus originated.

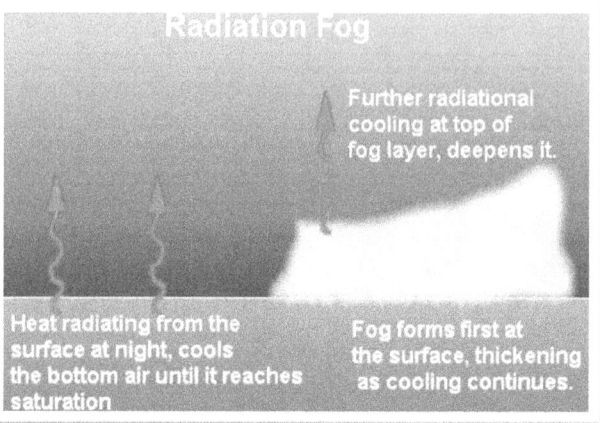

Fig.8.1: Radiation fog

2. **Advection fog:** It is formed due to mixing of warm moist air and cold air due to arrival of warm and moist air over cold ground surface. Dense advection fogs are also formed when cold and warm current converge.

Example dense fogs formed near Japanese coast when cools Kwille and warm Kuroshi currents converge.

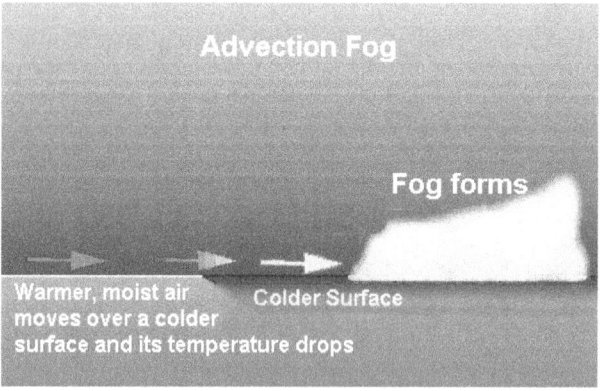

Fig.8.2: Advection fog

3. **Frontal fog:** Frontal fog (or precipitation fog) forms as precipitation falls into drier air below the cloud, the liquid droplets evaporate into water

132

vapor. The water vapor cools and at the dew point it condenses and fog forms.

This is formed when two contrasting air masses (warm and cold air masses) converge. When warm air, which is lighter pushed upward by cold air hence warm air is cooled from below dew to underlying cold air and fog originated after condensation (see the following fig.53).

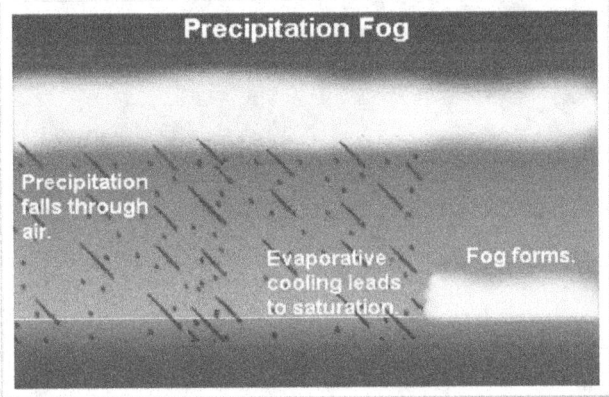

Fig.8.3: Frontal fog

4. **Steam fog:** It is formed when cold air passes over a much warmer water surface. So, water vapour due to the evaporation of warm water surface rises as a steam and condenses after meeting cold air above to form fog. This fog is known as **"evaporation fog"**.

Fig.8.4: Steam fog

133

5. **Hill fog:** Also this known as *upslope fog* that formed when winds blow air up a slope (called orographic uplift). The air cools as it rises, allowing moisture in it to condense.

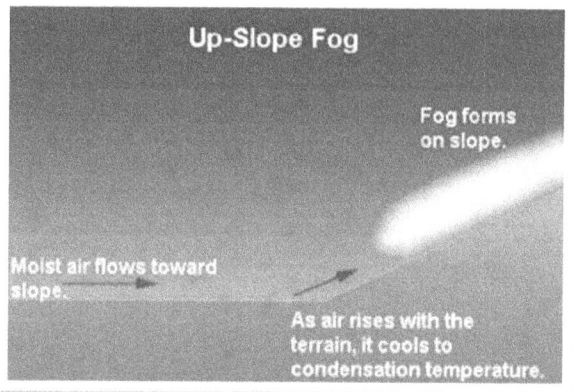

Fig.8.5: Hill fog

6. **Freezing fog:** Freezing fog is composed of super cooled water droplets which remain liquid even though the temperature is below freezing-point. One of the characteristics of freezing fog is that rime - composed of feathery ice crystals - is deposited on the windward side of vertical surfaces such as lamp posts, fence posts, overhead wires, pylons and transmitting masts.

Fig.8.6: Freezing fog

134

7. *Valley fog:* It is most common on a clear, calm night during the late night and early morning hours. Rivers and streams that flow in the base of valleys can also enhance the fog potential because of the relatively warm water of these bodies of water.

If the air temperature around a river or stream cools down to or below the temperature of the water, an instance source of condensation and water vapor becomes available for the production of fog.

Visibility as a result of valley fog can drop from unrestricted across higher terrain down to near zero miles in just a few hundred feet! Valley fog can also make for some picturesque scenery during the morning hours as the sun is rising.

Fig.8.7: Valley fog

8. *Ice fog:* Forming in very low temperatures can be the result of other mechanisms mentioned here, as well as the exhalation of moist warm air by herds of animals. It can be associated with the diamond dust form of precipitation, in which very small crystals of ice form and slowly fall.

This often occurs during blue sky conditions which can cause many types of halos and other results of refraction of sunlight by the airborne crystals (see the following fig.58).

Fig.8.8: Ice fog

9. ***Hail fog:*** Hail fog sometimes occurs in the vicinity of significant hail accumulations due to decreased temperature and increased moisture leading to saturation in a very shallow layer near the surface. It most often occurs when there is a warm, humid layer at the hail and when wind is light.

This ground fog tends to be localized but can be extremely dense and abrupt. It may formed shortly after the hail falls; when the hail has had time to cool the air and as it absorbs heat when melting and evaporating.

2. CLOUDS.

Clouds are defined as aggregate (accumulation) of tiny water droplets, ice particles, or mixture of both in the air above the ground surface. Clouds are the floating separate masses of water vapour suspended in the atmosphere cooling down to the dew point and type water droplets or size crystals, are formed.

Clouds are formed due to condensation of water vapour around hydroscopic nuclei caused by cooling due to lifting of air. Meteorologically clouds are very important because all forms of precipitation occur from clouds. Therefore, clouds are formed when air containing water vapour (saturated air) cools down to or below dew point and water vapour condense into water droplets or ice crystals. The following are point to note about clouds:

1. When air is cooled, some of its water vapour may condense into type water droplets. Before this happens, air must be saturated.

2. The temperature at which water droplets are formed is called dew point temperature.

3. Sometimes condensation takes place out seas or directly on the surface of the grounds. Water droplets formed here are called dew. Dew formed at night and helps to keep plants alive especially in the arid and semi-arid regions and in other regions during dry season.

4. Sometimes condensation of water in the air may lead to the formation of mist and fog which are made of condensed water vapour formed very near to the earth's surface. However mist and fog are forms of clouds.

5. The shape, height and movements of clouds determine to the large extent the sky, condition and the weather condition of a place in question. On statistical maps the place with equal/degree of cloudiness are joined by the lines called *isonephs.*

Classification of Clouds and Their Characteristics
There is variation of clouds in terms of height, shape, colour, transmission and reflection capacity, but common classification of clouds it is based on the height where clouds originated and appearance (texture) from the ground.

However; general classification of clouds (as proposed by Lake Howard (1803)) bases on their **appearance**, **form** and **height**. Howard used four Latin words to serve the purpose of cloud classification. These clouds include:
 * *Cirrus (Cirro = curl of hair, high)*
 * *Nimbus (Nimbo = rain, precipitation)*
 * *Cumulus (Cumulo = heap)*
 * *Stratus (Strato = layer)*

Through the four names of clouds, he also compiled composite names by using the four terms, e.g. Cumulonimbus, Cirrostratus etc.

General Classification of Clouds Based On Height
Clouds are classified according to their height above and texture from the ground as clarified in the following ways:

(a) High Clouds (Height 6000-12000m).
These types of clouds are found or formed in the height of 6000 to 12000 meters above the ground in the blue sky. Here also there are other types of clouds as the three main types of high-level clouds:

137

1. *Cirrus clouds:* are geniuses of atmospheric clouds generally characterized by thin, feathery, wispy strands, and composed entirely of ice crystals giving the type their name from the Latin word *"Cirrus"* meaning ringlet or curling lock of hair (see the following fig.59)

Fig.8.9: Cirrus clouds

2. *Cirrocumulus clouds:* These appear white globular (shape like a ball) masses forming ripples. They are layered clouds permeated with small cumuliform lumpiness. They also may line up in *streets/rows* of clouds across the sky denoting localized areas of ascent (cloud axes) and descent (cloud-free channels).

Fig.8.10: Cirrocumulus clouds:

3. *Cirrostratus clouds:* These are found under cirrocumulus, which resemble the thin white sheet, and the sky in this looks milky. They form a widespread, veil-like layer similar to what stratus clouds do in low levels. As a warm front approaches, cirrus clouds tend to thicken

into cirrostratus, which may, in turn thicken and lower into altostratus, stratus and even nimbostratus.

Fig.8.11: Cirrostratus clouds

(b) Middle Clouds (2000-600m)

These are middle-level clouds which occur at the height of above 2000 – 600 meters above the ground. These clouds may be composed of liquid water droplets, ice crystals, or a combination of two, including super-cooled droplets. Under this category there are:

1. *Altocumulus clouds*: These are wooly bumpy clouds. They are arranged in layer like waves and indicate fire weather.

   Altocumulus clouds with some vertical extend may denote the presence of elevated instability, especially in the morning, which could become boundary-layer, based and is released into deep convection during the afternoon or evening time (see the following fig.62).

Fig.8.12: Altocumulus clouds

139

2. *Altostratus clouds:* These are denser greenish clouds with water's look. They have a striated structure through which sun's rays shove friendly. Altostratus clouds themselves do not produce significant precipitation at the surface, although sprinkle or occasionally light showers may occur from a thick altostratus deck.

Fig.8.13: Altostratus clouds:

(c) Low Clouds (Height Up To 600m)

These clouds are found at about 600 meters above the surface of the ground. Low-level clouds are not given a prefix, although their names are derived from *"strato"* or "cumulo" depending on their characteristics. Have the following types:

1. *Stratocumulus clouds:* Are rough-bumpy clouds with pronounced waves than Altocumulus. Stratocumulus clouds are hybrids of layered stratus and cellular cumulus. Stratocumulus appears frequently in the atmosphere, either ahead of or behind a frontal system.

Fig.8.14: Stratocumulus clouds

2. *Stratus clouds:* Stratus clouds mean rain if it is warm and snow if it is cold. They look like a huge gray blanket that hangs low in the sky. Sometimes stratus clouds are on the ground or very near the ground, and then we call them fog. They Appears like a high land, thus reduced visibility of the air craft.

Fig.8.15: Stratus clouds:

3. *Nimbostratus clouds:* They Are clouds bringing continuous rainfall and snow. They are dark, dull and clearly layered.

Fig.8.16: Nimbostratus clouds:

4. *Cumulus clouds:* Cumulo- means "heap" or "pile" in Latin. Cumulus clouds are often described as "puffy", "cotton-like" or "fluffy" in appearance, and have flat bases **Cumulus clouds** are puffy **clouds** that sometimes look like pieces of floating cotton. The base of each **cloud** is often flat and may be only 1000 meters (3300 feet) above the ground. The top of the **cloud** has rounded towers.

141

Fig.8.17: Cumulus clouds

5. *Cumulonimbus clouds:* Cumulonimbus, from the Latin cumulus ("heap") and nimbus ("rainstorm", "storm cloud"), is a dense towering vertical cloud associated with thunderstorms and atmospheric instability, forming from water vapor carried by powerful upward air currents.

Fig.8.18: Cumulonimbus clouds

Description of Clouds' Form According to the World Meteorological Organization (WMO)

The World Meteorological Organization (WMO) is an intergovernmental organization with a membership of 191 Member States and Territories. It originated from the International Meteorological Organization (IMO), which was founded in 1873. Established in 1950, WMO became the specialized agency of the United Nations for meteorology (weather and climate), operational hydrology and related geophysical sciences.

It has its headquarters in Geneva, Switzerland, and is a member of the United Nations Development Group. The current Secretary-General is Petteri

142

Taalas. The current president is David Grimes. WMO have classified clouds into the following five categories:

1. **Cirrus clouds:** They are hair like clouds or silky appearance. They are composed of tiny ice crystal and they are transparent and while in clour.

2. **Cirrocumulus clouds:** They are white coloured clouds having patched which are arranged in distinct groups or wave like form.

3. **Altostratus clouds:** They are thin sheets of gray or blue color having fibrous or uniform appearance. When they become thick sheet, the sun and moon are obscured.

4. **Cumulus clouds:** They are very denser wide spread and dome shaped and have flat bases. They are white wool pack cloud masses.

5. **Cumulonimbus clouds:** They show great vertical development and normally produces heavy rains, snow or hail storm accompanied by lightening.

Note: take a note that, there are some other minor types of clouds like: *well clouds, Shelf clouds, Fractus clouds, Mammatus clouds, contrail clouds* and *Fog clouds.*

3. RAIN FALL

Rainfall is one of the precipitation whereby water droplets falls from high in the atmosphere into the earth's surface. Rainfall occurs when the water droplets in the clouds **coalesce** into large drops between **0.2mm** and **6mm** which is too heavy to remain in the atmosphere.

The presence of warm, moist and unstable air sufficient, numbers of hygroscopic nuclei are prerequisite condition for rainfall. The warm and moist air being lifted upward becomes saturated and clouds are formed which results rain.

Types of Rainfall

Rainfall as rain, or the amount of rain that falls have the following main three identified types:

(a) Convection rainfall

(b) Cyclonic/Convergent/Front rainfall

(c) Relief/Orographic rainfall

(a) Convection Rainfall

Convectional rainfall is common in the tropics where there is intensive heating during the day and in temperate interiors. This rainfall is associated with thunder and lightning. In temperate regions, thunders are there but occasional.

Therefore, convectional rainfall occurs due to thermal convectional current caused by heating of the ground surface. The cumulonimbus clouds are formed in this type of rainfall. *In this rainfall, two conditions are necessary to cause convectional rainfall:*

(a) Abundant supply of moisture through evaporation into the air.

(b) Intense heating of the ground surface through incoming solar radiations. So when the air coming into contact with warm ground surface, also get heated, becomes warm, expands and ultimately rise upward. The ascending warm and moisture air reach dew point form, consequently rainfall occurs.

Convectional current characterized by the following:
1. Occurs daily in the afternoon in the equatorial region.
2. It is of very short duration but occurs in the form of heavy showers.
3. It occurs through thick, dark and extensive cumulonimbus cloud.
4. It's accompanied by cloud thunder of lighting.
5. It supports luxurious evergreen rain forest in the equatorial regions.
6. Convectional rain is not regular in hot desert but is irregular and sudden (torrential rain).

(b) Orographic Rainfall.

This type of rainfall occurs due to ascending air forced by mountain barriers. The moist ascending air will continue to rise until they reach dew point and condensation occurs around hygroscopic nuclei. The slopes of the mountain facing the wind are called **windward side** (slope) and receive maximum rainfall. While the opposite slope is called **leeward slope** (side) receive very little rainfall.

This rainfall is caused by convectional currents. Orographic rainfall occurs when the moist air (saturated) or near saturated is forced to rise where confronted by a coasted or a near coastal mountain burners. It is best developed on the windward side of the sea or ocean. Here the air is forced to rise and cools down in the higher altitude, where condensation takes place forming clouds and rains.

Since this rainfall is caused by the relief of the land, it is also called **relief rainfall**. Example of such rainfall occurs in the north-earth slopes of Peninsular, Malaysia, Western Newzealand, Western Scotland, Asia hill of India, Bangladesh and Eastern sides of Drakensberg Mountains in South Africa. The leeward side forms rain shadow where there is little or no precipitation at all.

Conditions for formation of orographic rainfall:
1. There should be mountain barrier across the wind direction.
2. There should be sufficient amount of moisture content in the air.
3. The height of the mountains also affects the form and amount of orographic rainfall.

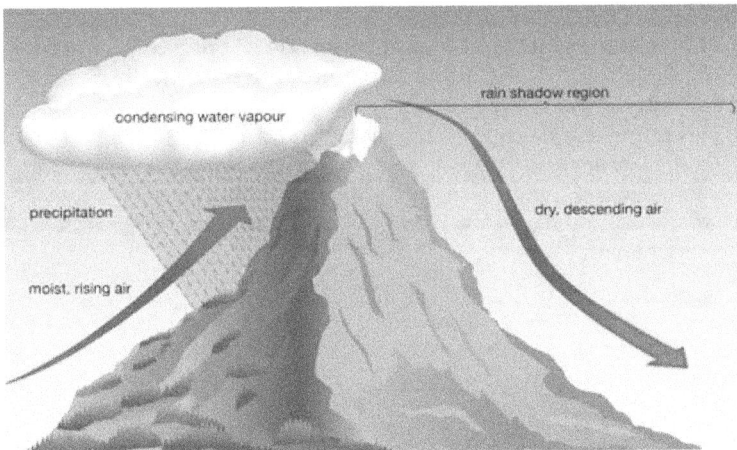

Fig.8.19: Orographic rainfall

Orographic Rainfall Characterized By the Following Characteristics:
1. The windward slope receives maximum rainfall whereas leeward (slope) experience very little rainfall.

2. There is a maximum rainfall near the mountain slopes and it decrease away from the foot hill.

3. Orographic rainfall may occur in any season while other types of rainfall they depend on climatic condition and seasons.

4. The windward slopes of the mountain at the time of rainfall are characterized by Cumulus clouds while leeward have Stratus clouds.

(c) *Cyclonic or Frontal Rainfall*

This type of rain occurs when warm and moist air masses forced to rise after converging with cold and dense air masses. Therefore, the warm air lying over the cold air is cooled and gets saturated and condensation begins around hygroscopic nuclei.

This type of rainfall is purely associated by cyclonic activities there in temperate regions (depression) or in tropical regions (cyclones), where westerlies and polar winds converge and around ITCZ and where North East and South East trade winds meet.

Conditions for frontal rainfall to occur:
- ☑ Two air masses meet, one a warm air mass and one a cold air mass.
- ☑ The lighter, less dense, warm air is forced to rise over the denser, cold air.
- ☑ This causes the warm air to cool and begin to condense.
- ☑ As the warm air is forced to rise further condensation occurs and rain is formed.
- ☑ Frontal rain produces a variety of clouds, which bring moderate to heavy rainfall.

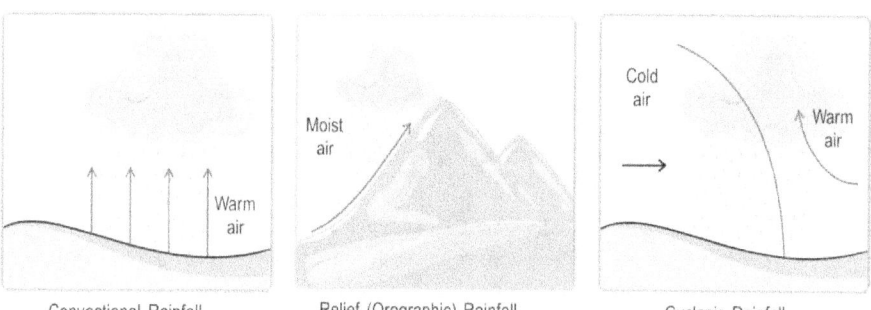

Convectional Rainfall   Relief (Orographic) Rainfall   Cyclonic Rainfall

Fig.8.20: Three types of rainfall

Other Forms of Precipitation:

01. *SNOW:* Snow is formed when water vapor condenses at a temperate below freezing-point passing directly from the gaseous to solid state and forming minute speckles of ice.

02. *SLEET:* In United Kingdom sleet refers to a mixture of snow and rain, but in America sleet means falling of small pallets of transparent having a diameter below 50mm.

03. *HAIL:* Hail consists of large pallets of ice. These pallets normally known as hail stones having diameter of 50mm. Hail are very destructive because they destroy agricultural crops.

04. *DRIZZLE:* The fall of numerous uniform minutes' droplets of water having diameter of less than 0.5mm. Drizzle fall continuously from low stratus clouds.

Hydrological Cycle (Water Cycle)

Hydrological cycle is the endless or continuous interchange of water between the atmosphere, the earth (land) and water bodies. It is the circulation of water from ocean into the atmosphere through combined effects of evaporation, transpiration, condensation and precipitation.

Evaporation: The process in which liquid water turn into water vapor and rises up.

Transpiration: The loss of water vapor fr

om plants in the form of vapor to the atmosphere.

Condensation: The process in which water vapor turns into the liquid form following a drop in atmospheric temperature. The temperature at which condensation takes place is called *dew point.* The dew point is the temperature at which the water vapor in air at constant barometric pressure condenses into liquid.

Precipitation: This refers to any product of condensation of atmospheric water vapor that fall under gravity. The main forms of precipitation include drizzle, rain, sleet, snow, hail and graupel. Precipitation occurs when a portion of the atmosphere becomes saturated with water vapor, so that the water condenses and "precipitates"(see the following fig. 8.21).

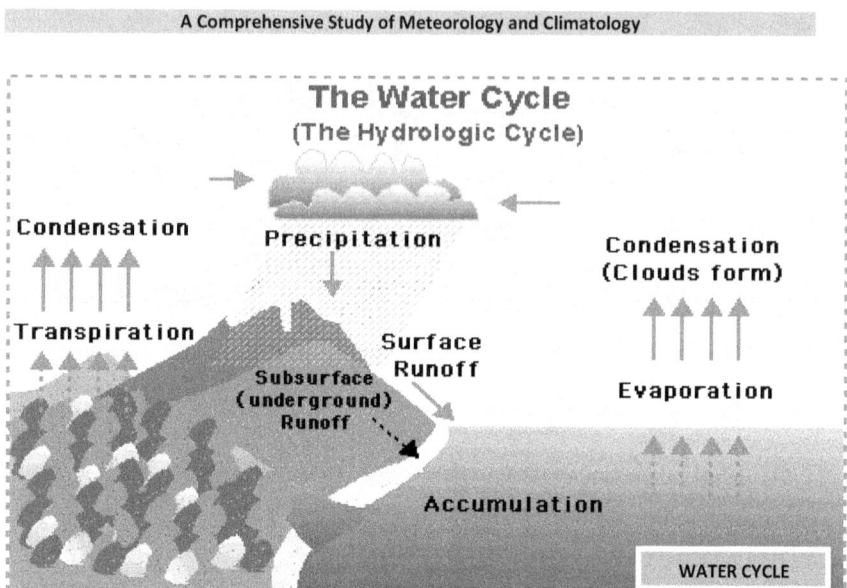

Fig.8.21: Hydrological cycle

CHAPTER NINE

OCEAN CURRENTS

Surface ocean currents correspond roughly to wind direction patterns because the winds of the world set ocean currents in the motion. By definition, oceanic current is the movement of oceanic water from high density concentrated to the low density content ratio. In other way, an ocean current is any more or less permanent or continuous, directed movement of ocean water that flows in one of the earth's oceans.

In other way, ocean currents can be defined as the vertical and horizontal movement of both surface and deep water throughout the world's oceans. The difference of air pressure causes wind movement and the difference in density causes oceanic movement. The currents are generated from the forces acting upon the water like the earth's rotation, the wind, the temperature and salinity differences and the gravitation of the moon.

When water evaporates, the density of water increase for the deposition (accumulation) of unevaporates minerals, such as salt, residues and other minerals. In that area the water becomes very denser. High density of water exists in the area of high pressure where descending warm air pick up the moisture plentiful, the density of the ocean is low. So, these differences in density in the oceanic water cause the movement of water from one part to another.

Ocean currents are similar to winds in the atmosphere in that they transfer significant amounts of heat from earth's equatorial areas to the poles and thus play important roles in determining the climates of coastal regions. In addition, ocean currents and circulation influence one another. The general circulation of the oceans defines the average movement of seawater, which, like the atmosphere, follows a specific pattern.

Superimposed on this pattern are oscillations of tides and waves, in which are not considered part of the general circulation. There also are meanders and eddies that represent temporal variations of the general circulation.

The ocean circulation pattern exchanges water of varying characteristics, such as temperature and salinity, within the interconnected network of oceans and is an important part of the heat and freshwater fluxes of the global climate. Horizontal movements are called currents, which range in magnitude from a few centimeters per second to as much as 4 meters (about 13 feet) per second.

A characteristic surface speed is about 5 to 50 cm (about 2 to 20 inches) per second. Currents generally diminish in intensity with increasing depth. Vertical movements often referred to as *up-welling* and *down-welling*, exhibit much lower speeds, amounting to only a few meters per month. As seawater is nearly incompressible, vertical movements are associated with regions of convergence and divergence in the horizontal flow patterns.

Oceanic currents affect not only the temperature of the area but also the precipitation on land areas adjacent to the ocean. A cold oceanic current near the land masses cause air just above the water to be cold while air above is warm. This brings little opportunity of convection to bring moisture to the land, so rainfall is very little. Warm oceanic currents near the land mass cause air just above the water to be warm, while air above is warm.

So convectional rainfall is very high to occur and heavy rain is obtained to the coastal or land such as those in coastal area of India. Each major current can be characterized as warm or cool relative to the surrounding water at the latitude:

- ☑ California current (cool),
- ☑ Equatorial current (warm),
- ☑ West wind drift (cool),
- ☑ Humboldt Current (cool),
- ☑ Gulf Stream (warm),
- ☑ Labrador Current (cool),
- ☑ North Atlantic drift (warm),
- ☑ Canary's current (cool),
- ☑ Brazil current (warm),
- ☑ Benguela current (cool),
- ☑ West Austrian current (cool),
- ☑ East Australia current (warm),
- ☑ Kuroshio current (warm),
- ☑ Oyashio current (cool) *and*
- ☑ North pacific drift (warm).

A summary of Causes of Ocean Currents

Ocean currents are the outcome of the interaction of a number of factors which include:

The earth's rotation: This determines the direction of the ocean currents because it influences the direction of wind through the coriolis forces. Therefore, ocean currents flow in direction to the right in the Northern hemisphere and the left in Southern hemisphere.

Difference in ocean water salinity: This is the concentration of soluble salts in waters of the oceans. High concentration of salinity leads to dense water with low level of salinity to occupy.

The effects of water temperature differences: The difference in water temperature affects the density of water the density of the water. Therefore, cold water in the poles is heavy and so it sinks, leaving a space to be occupied by water that has expanded from the tropics; hence warm water from the poles forms deep or submarine currents.

Prevailing winds: These are winds which blow constantly over a certain surface for a long time. As the winds blow over the water surface it produces a dragging effect such as the water moves towards the same direction as that of wind. For example the monsoon winds tend to cause the drift currents like North Atlantic drift.

The topography of the sea floor and the shape of the ocean's basins: This affects both the surface and deep ocean currents as they restrict areas where water can move and funnel it into another.

Shape of the land masses: This influences the movement of ocean currents; in that, the currents tend to flow following the coastline. Land masses may also split a current into two, affecting its direction e.g. the Madagascar Island splits the equatorial current into two.

Types of Oceanic Currents and their Global Distribution:

1. *Cold oceanic currents.*

These are those oceanic currents originated from cold oceanic water. Cold oceanic currents are mostly found on coastal desert of the world; examples Canary and Banguela currents in Africa, Califonia and Labrador currents in North America and Peru currents in South America, East green land current in Europe.

2. *Warm oceanic currents.*

They are among of those oceanic currents originated from warm oceanic water. Example Guinea and Angulhas currents in Africa, Florida, Gulf Stream in North America, Brazil current in South America, West Green land current in Europe (see the following map in fig.72).

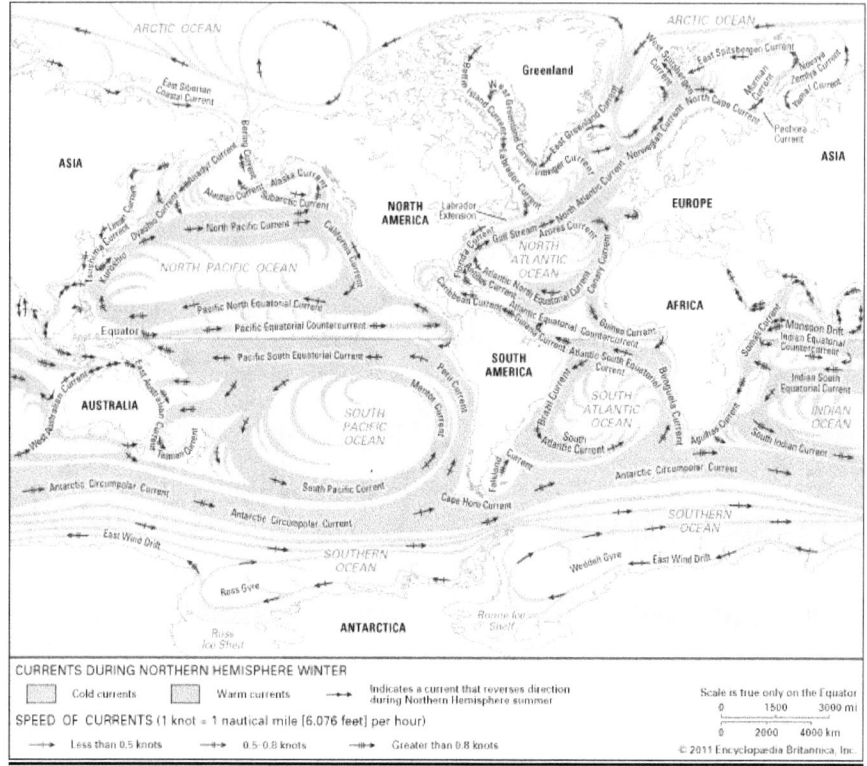

Fig.9.1: Global distributions of ocean currents (source Encyclopedia Britannica 2011)

CHAPTER TEN

CLIMATE AND CLIMATOLOGY

1. CLIMATOLOGY

Climatology (from Greek *klima*, "place, zone"; and *-logia*) is the study of climate, scientifically defined as weather conditions averaged over a period of time. This modern field of study is regarded as a branch of the atmospheric sciences and a subfield of physical geography, which is one of the Earth sciences.

Climatology now includes aspects of oceanography and biogeochemistry. The gaseous envelop surrounding the earth is called atmosphere while the science dealing with the study of the atmospheric components and characteristics is called *meteorology* and *climatology.*

Approaches or Principles of climatology

Climatology is principled or approached in a variety of ways like in the following:

1. *Paleoclimatology*: seeks to reconstruct past climates by examining records such as ice cores and tree rings (dendroclimatology).

2. *Paleotempestology*: uses the same records to help determine hurricane frequency over millennia. The study of contemporary climates incorporates meteorological data accumulated over many years, such as records of rainfall, temperature and atmospheric composition.

   Knowledge of the atmosphere and its dynamics is also embodied in models, either statistical or mathematical, which help by integrating different observations and testing how they fit together. Modeling is used for understanding past, present and potential future climates.

3. *Historical climatology* is the study of climate as related to human history and thus focuses only on the last few thousand years.

The Differences between Climatology (Climatologists) and Meteorology (Meteorologists)

In contrast to meteorology, which focuses on short term weather systems lasting up to a few weeks, climatology studies the frequency and trends of those systems. It studies the periodicity of weather events over years to millennia, as well as changes in long-term average weather patterns, in relation to atmospheric conditions. Climatology considers the past and can help predict future climate change.

Both climatology and meteorology are branches of physical science that deal with the weather. While they are related to one another in many ways, they are not the same thing. Weather changes frequently, but the climate is relatively stable. The major difference between the two sciences is basically the time.

Climatologists and meteorologists are two types of atmospheric scientists who study weather patterns and their effects on humans and the environment. A key difference relates to time horizons. Meteorologists focus more on short-term weather conditions while climatologists are more interested in long-term climate conditions. More recently, the issue of global warming has become a source of disagreement between climatologists and meteorologists.

Features: Climatologists and meteorologists both use radar and satellite data, as well as sophisticated computer models, to study atmospheric conditions. The U.S. Bureau of Labor Statistics identifies two types of meteorologists: broadcast meteorologists, who prepare and deliver weather forecasts on radio and television news programs, and research meteorologists, who generally work for government agencies and colleges, collecting and analyzing weather data and producing forecasts.

Climatologists, also known as climate scientists, study current and historical weather conditions to project long-term trends, such as shifts in temperature or precipitation, according to the BLS. Most climatologists work for the government, scientific research firms and institutes of higher education.

Differences: A key difference between meteorologists and climatologists lies in the time perspectives they bring to the study of weather and climate. Meteorologists produce forecasts that are intended to predict weather conditions over the short term, often a horizon no longer than 7 to 10 days.

Climatologists, meanwhile, employ a long-term perspective, developing and analyzing models that are designed to predict changes in weather patterns in the months and years to come. A meteorologist will predict whether it will rain in the next day or two, but a climatologist will predict whether climate patterns will result in more rainfall on average in the years to come.

Equipment: Meteorologists and climatologists use much of the same equipment, but in different ways. Here we look at specific instruments and how each discipline uses them.

Satellites: Along with radar, satellites are among the most sophisticated and expensive equipment used in atmospheric science. For meteorologists, satellites provide two useful pieces of information. First and foremost, they allow for weather tracking on a large scale and over time. The large "view" of satellites is what allows us to track hurricanes, El Nino events, and other large weather patterns. Though not perfect, satellites increase hurricane (typhoon) warnings from hours to days and provide weather information that stretches out over roughly a week for any particular location in the world.

The second use of satellites in meteorology is in atmospheric data collection that helps guide predictions. Things like temperature, barometric pressure, and more are collected by satellites and then used in models to make short-term (usually 10 days at most) predictions about weather.

Climatologists make very different use of satellites because they are less interested in day-to-day changes or in tracking specific storms. To climatologists, satellites offer important data about physical processes occurring at different levels of the atmosphere. These processes would be difficult or impossible to track by other means, though weather balloons are still used to some extent.

Satellites, for instance, can be used to track temperature at various levels and follow convective currents to learn how energy is circulated within the atmosphere. Satellites can also be used to track climate indices like the North Atlantic Oscillation and measure things like sea level rise and ice coverage, all of which are critical to understanding long-term trends in Earth's weather.

Radar: Radar is a major piece of atmospheric equipment, with most units costing tens of millions of dollars (USD). Many people are probably familiar with Doppler radar, which allows meteorologists to track storms in high detail and make predictions about things like tornado touchdown probabilities, rainfall amounts, storm tracks, etc.

Radar is less useful to climatologists because it is used for minute-to-minute observation of the weather, but that does not mean it is entirely useless to them. Pressure data, wind data, and other information collected over long periods of time by radar can be combined with things like satellite data to

155

understand how upper-level atmospheric phenomena relate to surface phenomena.

Scale (Keep a note about Scale): Scale is not a useful way to distinguish meteorology from climatology unless the scale is applied to time. In terms of area, though, the two overlap too much to make scale a useful method of distinction. Atmospheric science divides scale into four main categories:

1) *Microscale* – Areas of 1 km or less. This usually falls under the domain of meteorology as it is mostly concerned with tracking individual storms, etc. However, urban climatologists may concern themselves with small areas, even down to individual city blocks.

2) *Mesoscale* – This is the study of scales in two different directions, horizontal and vertical. Horizontal areas (surface areas) ranging from the microscale below to the synoptic scale at the upper bound. Vertical scaling includes all layers of the Earth's atmosphere except the upper stratosphere.

3) *Synoptic Scale* – This is the study of large things like jet streams, frontal zones, and cyclones. Satellite data is virtually essential to studies done at this scale.

4) *Global scale* – Just like it sounds, this is the study of weather patterns over the entire globe. While it may seem that this would be the sole domain of climatologists, remember that meteorologists are also interested in things like the El Nino-Southern Oscillation because it directly impacts weather predictions.

Branches of Climatology

Climatology is classified into the followings types or there are three branches of climatology which are:

(i)   Physical climatology
(ii)   Regional climatology
(iii)   Applied climatology.

1. Physical Climatology.

Physical climatology deals with the occurrence of the climatic condition of the place of how rain formed and why wind blow. It studies various elements of weather namely insolation, temperature, precipitation, fogs, visibility etc. it is thus, evident that physical climatology studies the factors and process of regional of climatic conditions.

2. *Regional Climatology.*

Regional climatology deals with the characteristics and variation of climatic condition from one place to another. E.g. why equatorial region receives heavy rainfall? Why there is a high temperature in desert areas? Regional climatology includes the study of types, distribution, patterns and characteristics factors of world climates. Regional climatology is studies in three ways on the basis of spatial scale viz: *Macro-climatic region*, *Meso-climatic region* and *Micro-climatic region.*

3. *Applied Climatology.*

It is the branch of climatology which deals with showing the relationship between climatology and other scientific subject like physics, chemistry and biology among others.

Applied climatology studies the application of climatic knowledge to solve various problems faced by human society e.g. global warming and climate changes. It studies the interactions between climate and biosphere i.e. how does climate influence and control plants and animals including man and in turn how does man modify climate by introducing advertent and advertent changes in physical environment and by making certain weather modification e.g. cloud seeding and induced precipitation

2. CLIMATE

Climate refers to the atmospheric weather condition observed, measured and recorded over a considerable long period of time; normally over 30 years. Climate in a wider sense is the state, including a statistical description, of the climate system. The climate of a location is affected by its latitude, terrain, and altitude, as well as nearby water bodies and their currents. Climates can be classified according to the average and the typical ranges of different variables, most commonly temperature and precipitation.

Classification of Climates

Classification of climate refers to an attempt to simplify by identifying the categories of climate patterns with the same characteristics. Also refers to as the process of grouping the variation of geographical unit with similar climate characteristics into classes. The study of climate is also divided into three types based on influences of climatic environment on human health and behavior of different spatial scale viz:

1. *Micro-climate:* Micro-climate, which represents weather conditions surrounding an individual organism.

2. *Eco-climate:* Ecological climate or eco-climate, which represents weather elements of habitats of the organisms, in the case of man the habitat may his house and working places like factory, office, mine, agricultural farm, pasture and alike.

3. *Geo-climate:* Geographical or geo-climate, which represents weather conditions of large areal unit and large temporal span.

Qn: 1. Discuss for the factors affecting climate
2. How climate influence on life, environment and economic activities?

Some Climatologists with their Systems

The earliest attempt of climatic classification where made by Greek Philosophers, who divided the world into three latitudinal zones, namely: **torrid;** which based on within the tropics, **temperate;** considered in the middle latitudes and **frigid;** based on within the polar circles or regions. *Later, A. Miller, W. Köppen* among others they attempted to give out the systems of classification. Köppen classification system is the most and widely used in Africa and the world in general.

1. Wlandimir Köppen System

The system divided the climate into five major groups of climates based on temperature, precipitation and division of natural vegetation as follows:

A. *Tropical Moisture Climate:* It is also known as *tropical rain forest.* Have an average temperature of 18°C in all months, no real winter season.

B. *Dry Climate:* Have dry climate with low rainfall during most of the year. In this, potential evaporation and transpiration exceed precipitation.

C. *Moist Mid-latitude Climate with Mild winter.* Warm to hot summer with mild winter. The average temperature is 18°C and 3°C above. It is also known as *warm temperate rainy climate.*

D. *Moist Mid-latitude Climate with Severe Winter.* It is also called *cold snowy forest climate.* The average temperature of the warmest month is 10⁰C and above, the coldest monthly averages drops below -3⁰C.

E. *Polar Climate:* Extremely cold in winter and summer and there is real summer season. The average temperature of the warmest is below 10⁰C.

Major and Minor Groups of the Köppen System of Climate Classification

Na.	Climatic groups	Symbol	Dry period	Degree of dryness and coldness
01.	Tropical moist climates	A	f(s)w	
02.	Dry climates	B		SW
03.	Warm moist mid-latitude climates	C	Fsw	
04.	Cold moist mid-latitude climates	D	f(s)w	
05.	Polar climates	E		TF

Table.10.1: Classification of major and minor groups of Köppen System of climate

Key to the letters from the table above:

* Small letter *(f, s and w)* indicate seasonal precipitation
* *(f)* Indicate no dry season
* *(s)* Indicate dry in to dry season
* *(w)* Indicate dry season in winter
* Capital letter *(S, W, T, and F)* indicate two subdivision of dry climate and polar climate
* *(S)* indicate semi-arid or steppe climate
* *(W)* Refers to arid or desert climate
* *(T)* Refers to tundra climate
* *(F)* Refers to frozen or ice carp climate

*The general combination of the major five (5) climates and the subdivision (minor) climates of the **Köppen system climate classification**, involve the following eleven (11) climatic types:*

159

1. **'Af'** = Tropical climate with no dry season
2. **'Aw'** = Tropical climate with winter dry season
3. **'BS'** = Steppe dry climate
4. **'BW'** = Desert dry climate
5. **'Cf'** = Mild climate with no dry season
6. **'Cs'** = Mild climate with dry season
7. **'Cw'** = Mild climate with dry winter
8. **'Df'** = Micro climate with no dry season
9. **'Dw'** = Micro climate with dry winter
10. **'ET'** =Tundra cold climate
11. **'Ef'** = Snow-ice climate

Distribution of Köppen System Climates
The distribution of climatic types by Köppen system can be shown as follows:

A: *Tropical Moist Climates:*
These extend northwards and southwards from the equator to about 15^0 or 25^0 of latitudes. All months have average temperature greater than 18^0C. Annual precipitation is greater than 1500mm. In this; there are three (3) minor seasonal distribution of rainfall:

(i). *Tropical Wet (Af):* It is the tropical climate in which the precipitation occurs all the year. Monthly temperature variations in this climatic region are less than 3^0C of the intense surface heating and high humidity, cumulus and cumulonimbus clouds from early in the afternoon almost every day. Daily temperatures are high, about 32^0C, while night temperature average is 22^0C.

(ii). *Tropical monsoon climate (Am):* It has annual rainfall which is equal or greater than **"Af"**, but most of the precipitation falls in the seven (7) and nine (9) hottest months. During the dry season, very little rainfall occurs.

(iii). *Tropical wet and dry or savanna (Aw):* Has an extended dry season during winter. Precipitation during the wet season is usually less than 1000mm and only wet during the summer season.

B: *Dry Climates:*
The most known features of these climates are that potential evaporation and transpiration exceed precipitation. These climates extends from 20^0C to 35^0C

north and south of the equator, an in the large continental regions of the mid-latitudes surrounded by mountains. Minor types of these climates are:

(i). *Dry arid or desert (BW):* it is a true desert climate which cover 12% of the earth's land surface, and it is dominated by *xerophytes* as a vegetation cover. This can be found in subtropics (BW*h*) and in the mid-latitudes (BW*k*).

(ii). *Dry semi-arid or steppe (BS):* It is a glass land climate that cover14% of the earth's land surface. It receives more precipitation than the desert. This found in subtropics (BS*h*) or mild-latitudes (BS*k*). The *h* indicates warm temperature, above (18⁰C) and represents the word *heiss* (means warm originating from German). The latter *k* if of German origin, representing the word *kalt* which means cold.

C: *Moist sub-tropical mid-latitude climates (Mesothermal):*
These warm temperate climates have generally warm and summer with mild winter. They exist between latitudes 30^0 to 50^0 north and south of the equator, mainly on the eater and western borders of most continents. During winter, the main weather features is the *mid-latitude cyclone*. Convective *thunderstorms* dominate the summer months. There are minor three in these:

(i). *Humid Subtropical (Cfa):* it has hot muggy summer and frequent thunderstorms, winters are mild and precipitation during the season comes from mid-latitude cyclones. The good example of *Cfa* climate is found in the southern east of USA.

(ii). *Marine climates (Cfb):* marine climates are found on the western coast of the continents. They have humid climate with short dry summer. Heavy precipitations occur during the winters because of the continuous presence of mid-latitude cyclones.

(iii). *Mediterranean climate (Cs):* Which receives rain fall form of precipitation during winter season from the mid-latitude cyclones. Summers are extremely dry due to the sinking of air of the sub-tropical highs and may exist for long up to five months. In Africa, this type of climate is found in the northern part bordering the Mediterranean Sea and the south western part of South Africa, while in North America it found in Portland, Oregon and California.

These types of climates (moist sub-tropical mid-latitude climates) can be grouped into other three types of climates as proposed by Faniran et al in 1980:

> *Cf* = Climates with no distinct dry season.
> *Cw* = climates with dry winter (like Monsoon in South East of Asia, North India and Southern China).
> *Cs* = Climates with dry summer which are Mediterranean.

D: *Moist continental mid-latitude climate (Micro thermal):*

These climates have warm to cool summer and cold winters. The location of these climates is pole wards of the *'C'* climates. The average temperatures of the warmest months are greater than 10°C, while the coldest months are lees that -30°C. Winters are severe with snowstorms, strong winds and bitter cold from continental polar or arctic air masses. Like *'C'* climates, it is subdivided into three minor types, which are:

(i). *Dry winters (Dw)*: like in north eastern Asia, where the winter anticyclones are well developed.

(ii). *Dry summer (S)*: it is dry in summer seasons and

(iii). *Cold and Wet (Df)*: humid all seasons. Important to note is, letter *'f'* represents climates which are wet with no dry season, while letter *'w'* refers to the climates with dry winter.

E: *Polar climates:*

Polar climates have year–around cold temperatures, with the warmest month having less than 10°C. Polar climates are found on the northern coastal areas of North America, Europe, Asia and all Greenland and Antarctica. There are two minor subdivisions in this climate:

(i). *Polar Tundra (ET)*: polar tundra climate is the climate in which the soil is permanently frozen to depths of hundreds of meters (the condition is known as *permafrost* or *perpetual frost*). Average temperature of the warmest is between 0°C to 10°C. Polar tundra occurs in northern parts of North America, north parts of Europe and the north parts of Asia. In these areas, vegetation is dominated by mosses, lichens, dwarf trees and scattered woody shrubs.

(ii). *Polar Ice caps (EF)*: has land surface that are permanently covered with snow and ice. The average temperatures of all the months are below 0°C. Green land and Antarctic have this type of climate. There is no vegetation cover on the land surface.

NOTE: Köppen classification system has greatly been modified. For example, *R. George* has added a latter *'H'* for highland climates.

Advantages of Köppen Classification System:

1. Has facilitated the study of climates to the geographers and alike in Africa and the world.

2. The study has facilitated the classification of various vegetation types in the world.

3. Due to its simplicity, the system is widely used in colleges and schools for various lessons in geographical and engineering activities.

4. It has stimulated studies and researches by various scholars, the characteristics of climates in different places and factors that control them.

5. The system has also given insight into the relationship between precipitation, temperature and vegetation.

Criticism against the Köppen System of Classification:

1. The divisions in climates are too abrupt while the changes on the surface occurs gradually because the climates are defined according to the fixed values of temperatures and precipitation hence computed basing to the averages for the year and for individual month.

2. The system is based on natural vegetation when classifying the climates makes the system to be not profound to the scientific purposes due to plant and vegetation growth are not influenced by precipitation and temperature, but there other factors like edaphic and physiographic factors.

3. His criteria proved unsatisfactory, since weaknesses have been noted between his climatic subdivisions and the features of natural landscape. For example, in the use of $-3^{0}C$ for boundary between the *'C'* and *'D'* climates has proved unsatisfactory in the USA where better results was obtained by using $0^{0}C$, while a value of $-50^{0}C$ was found more suitable in Europe. Therefore, these criteria are not uniformly applied in all places.

2. Climatic System According to Miller

Miller produced an important workable system of classification of great value to geographers because of its applicability to regional description, by combining a map zones to be the one, showing the seasonal distribution of rainfall. In his approach, he used temperature to identify the major groups and precipitation for the subdivisions. Miller classified climatic system into siding on temperature groups basing on vegetation zones as follow:

1. **Hot climates:** Always hot and no month below 18^0C.
   - ☑ *Equatorial with double maximum rain*
   - ☑ *Equatorial monsoon*
   - ☑ *Tropical marine with no marked dry season*
   - ☑ *Tropical marine (monsoon)*
   - ☑ *Tropical continental summer-rain*
   - ☑ *Tropical continental monsoon*

2. **Warm temperate climates:** no cold season, that is a month below 6^0C.
   - ☑ *Western margin (Mediterranean)*
   - ☑ *Eastern margin- uniform rain*
   - ☑ *Eastern margin (monsoon) – no marked summer maximum rain*

3. **Cold temperature climates:** cold season of one to five months below 6^0C.
   - ☑ *Marine uniform rain (winter maximum)*
   - ☑ *Continental-summer maximum rain*
   - ☑ *Continental monsoon with strong summer maximum rain*

4. **Cold climates:** long cold season of six months or more below 6^0C.
   - ☑ *Marine – uniform rain or winter maximum*
   - ☑ *Continental summer maximum rain*
   - ☑ *Continental monsoon with strong summer maximum rain*

5. **Very cold climate (Arctic):** no warm season; three months or less about 6^0C.

6. **Desert climates:** have less than 254mm of rainfall annually.
   - ☑ *Hot desert with no cold season; no month less than 6^0C*
   - ☑ *Middle latitudes desert with one or more months below 6^0C*

7. **Mountain climates:** specifically occur in the high lands and mountainous areas.

General Classification of Climates

Criteria for classifying climate include temperature, vegetation, humidity, solar radiation, altitude and physical of climate (like air mass), relief and soil. The world climate is neither uniform nor static. Climate conditions vary from one region to another throughout the world. Temperature and Rainfall are the most important elements determining climate. By combination, climate is grouped as follows:

(a) Hot Climate (Hot Zone).
1. *Equatorial climate.*
2. *Savannah (Tropical) Climate.*
3. *Tropical Maritime (Tropical Marine) Climate*
4. *Tropical Desert Climate.*
5. *Tropical Monsoon Climate.*

(b) Warm Climates.
1. *Mediterranean climate.*
2. *Warm temperature climate.*
3. *Warm temperature (interior climate).*

(c) Cool Climates.
1. *Cool temperature – West margin.*
2. *Cool temperature – East margin*

(d) Cold Climates
1. *Continental cold temperature climate*
2. *Tundra climate.*

(e) Very Cold Climate.
1. *Polar Climate.*
2. *Mountains climate.*

Without considering the grouping the types of climates; generally, the world's climates can be listed as follows:

1. Equatorial climate (Tropical rainforest climate)

2. Tropical (savannah) climate

3. Tropical desert climate

4. Warm temperate desert climate

5. Mediterranean climate (warm temperate western margin climate)

6. *Warm temperate continental climate*

7. *Warm temperate eastern margin climate.*

8. *Cool temperate western margin climate*

9. *Cool temperate continental climate*

10. *Cool temperate eastern margin climate*

11. *Cold temperate western margin climate*

12. *Cold temperate continental climate*

13. *Cold temperate eastern margin climate*

14. *Tundra climate*

15. *Polar climate*

16. *Mountain climate*

01.   Equatorial Climate

It is also known as Tropical rainforest climate. It occurs in latitudes between 5^0N and 5^0S of the equator. Sometimes may occur in latitude of 10^0 South and North of the equator. Example of regions in this climate are; in the area of Congo Basin in Africa and Amazon Basin in South America.

Characteristics of Equatorial climate:

(a) High temperatures throughout the year with an average of 27^0C and annual range of about 3^0C

(b) Heavy Rainfall throughout the year with double maxima

(c) Mean annual rainfall of 1500mm. Rainfall is very heavy and evenly distributed

(d) Rainfall is commonly convectional type of rainfall

(e) Lightning and thunderstorms are common

(f) Relative humidity is very high

(g) There are no seasons.

02.   Tropical (Savannah) Climate

It is found in latitudes between 5^0 and 15^0 on South and North of Equator.

Characteristic of Tropical climate:

(1) Temperate are high during the hot and dry seasons up to 32^0C

(2) During the coolest months, temperature drops to 21^0C

(3) Annual range of temperature is relatively high at 11^0C

(4) Temperature are highest just before the onset of the rainy season

(5) Rainfall is usually convectional type

(6) Presence of two seasons, the hot and dry seasons

(7) Rainfall is moderate and is higher near the areas that experience equatorial climate.

MONTH	J	F	M	A	M	J	J	A	S	O	N	D
TMP(°C)	22	22	21	18	18	16	16	18	22	24	24	22
RAIN(MM)	270	201	127	20	0	0	0	0	17	18	94	208

03.   Tropical Desert Climate

This occurs between 15^0 and 30^0 North and South of the equator. This commonly found in Namib Desert and Sahara Desert areas in African continent.

Characteristics of Tropical desert climate:

a) High mean monthly temperatures of 29°C during the hot season

b) During the cool season, temperatures can be as low as 10°C.

c) Day time temperatures can rise to 47°C or more.

d) Night temperature can drop to as low 5°C

e) Annual temperature range is very high. It can reach 26°C and diurnal range of temperature is approximately 40°C.

NONTHS	J	F	M	A	M	J	J	A	S	O	N	D
TEMP(°C)	10	13	16	20	25	30	33	32	28	22	16	11
RAIN (MM)	6	6	9	3	4	4	1	1	2	5	11	6

04.   Warm Temperate Desert Climate

It is also known as mid-latitude desert climate. Found in parts of South America, Eurasia (at Northern Syria, Northern Iran, Capsular and Aral areas), Mongolia (include the Gobi desert).

Characteristics of warm temperate desert climate:

(a) High summer temperature ranging between 25°C and 37°C

(b) Cold winter with temperature as low as 7°C

(c) Range of temperature is even larger, reaching 40°C

(d) Rainfall is low and unreliable due to the effect of continent.

167

05. Warm Temperate Western Margin (Mediterranean) Climate

It is locater between 30^0 and 45^0 on South and North of the side of the Equator. Mostly occurs on the Western sides of the continents particularly the lands bordering the Mediterranean Sea like Southern Europe and Northern Africa, Central coast of California South west Africa, coast of south west Australia and central Chile.

Characteristics of warm temperate western margin climate:

(a) Temperature range between 21^0C and 10^0C

(b) Summer season is hot and dry with cloudless skis

(c) During summer time humidity is low

(d) Winters are mild (cool) and wet

(e) The rainfall is between 500mm and 900mm and mainly of cyclonic type

06. Warm Temperate Continental Climate

This climate is also known as warm temperate interior climate. It is experienced in the interiors of continentals in the mid-latitudes between 30^0 and 50^0 North and South of the Equator.

Characteristics of warm temperate continental climate:

(a) Temperature range between 26^0C in summer and 10^0C in winter

(b) Annual range of temperature is moderate

(c) Mean annual rainfall varies between 380mm and 700mm depending on location.

(d) Rainfall is convectional types.

07. Warm Temperate Eastern Margin Climate

This is also known as china type. It occurs between 23^0 and 35^0 North and south of the Equator on the eastern side of the continents.

Characteristics of Temperate eastern Margin Climate:

(a) Hot summer with mean temperatures of 26^0C

(b) Mild to cool winters with mean temperature of 13^0C

(c) Mean annual Rainfall is about 1,000mm

(d) Monsoon winds have an influence on this climate in many areas except south America

(e) During summer, onshore trade wind are responsible for Rainfall

08.   Cool Temperate Western Margin Climate

This is also known as British type. It is experienced in areas bordering the west coast of continents.

Characteristics of cool temperate western margin climate:

(a) Warm summers with temperature varying between13⁰C and 15⁰C.

(b) Cool winters whose temperature vary between 2⁰C and 7⁰C

(c) Mean annual rainfall varies between 750mm and 2000mm.

09. Cool Temperate Continental Climates

This occurs in areas of the interior of North America and Europe. It is also known as cool temperate interior.

Characteristics of cool temperate continental climate:

a) Mild to warm summers with temperatures of up to 18⁰C

b) Very cold winters; sometimes temperature reach -19⁰C

c) Rainfall is low, between 400mm and 550mm and falls mainly is summer

10.   Cool Temperate Eastern Margin Climate

This also referred to as Laurentian type of climate. This climate is experienced in the eastern sides of North America and Asia.

Characteristics of cool temperate eastern margin climate:

a. Summers are warm with temperatures ranging between 12⁰C and 18⁰C

b. Temperatures range between 4⁰C and 15⁰C during winter

c. Annual range of temperature is very large up to -39⁰C

d. Precipitation is mainly in the form of rain with annual mean of between 700mm and 1000mm.

Activity: Discus for the cold temperate continental climate.

11. Cold Temperate Western Margin Climate

This one occurs in Alaska in North America and central and Northern Norway and Sweden

It has the following characteristics:

a. Short and cool summers with temperatures of 12⁰C on average

b. Winters are long with temperatures ranging between – 2⁰C and 4⁰C.

c. Temperatures are below 0°C for up to four (4) months

d. Rainfall comes in most of the months, but in winter it is in form of snow.

12. Cold Temperate Eastern Margin Climate

This climate is experienced in the North-East of Pacific Coast of Russia

It has the following characteristics:

a) Short but hot summers with mean temperature of 21°C or higher.

b) Winter are long and cold with temperatures dropping to 20°C

c) Cold temperatures are due to high pressure systems over Siberia

d) Annual rainfall totals vary between 1,000mm along the coast and 500mm in the interior

e) There is seasonal reversal of winds causing the climate to be referred to as Eastern margin mountain climate

f) Summers are wet while winters are dry.

13. Tundra Climate

This is the coastal region of North America bordering the Arctic Ocean. It includes Baffin Island and south coast of Greenland. In Eurasia, it occurs in the Arctic coastal region between Scandinavia and North east Russia.

14. Polar Climate

This climate occurs in the interior of Iceland, Greenland and Antarctic.

It is characterized by the followings:

(a) Very cold temperatures, permanently below 0°C

(b) Precipitation in form of snow and blizzards (snow storms) are frequent

(c) During winters, nights are continuous while in summer day is continuous

15. Mountain Climate

This is a climatic type which is common in the high mountain and high lands regions of the world.

Characteristics of Mountain Climate:

(a) Temperatures decrease with increasing altitude

(b) Rainfall increase with altitude and is orographic type.

(c) Windward slopes generally receive more rainfall than leeward slopes

(d) Maximum rainfall received is about 2500 mm after which it starts to decrease.

(e) Local winds are associated with temperature inversion.

Importance of Classifying Climate:

1. Helps in giving systematic description of a place, which in turn facilitates the planning process for social and economic activities.

2. Helps in marshaling large amount of data gathered from various geographical areas.

3. Helps in understanding the relationship between climate, vegetation, soil and other organism, and about how they influence each other.

4. Facilitate clear understanding for the global distribution of climates and therefore, geographers, sailors, pilots among others be aware over the global climates in general.

CHAPTER ELEVEN

NATURAL REGIONS

Climatic characteristics and types of vegetation can determine the types of mammal found and even the human activities that can take place in a certain area. Natural vegetation and animals that are found in a climate zone tend to share similar characteristics which by nature, differ from those found from other climate zone.

Example, animals found in hot climatic regions have short hairs while those found in cool or cold region normally have long hairs. Likewise, equatorial regions have huge and tall trees due to fast growing caused by high temperature and heavy rainfall throughout the year while semi-desert regions have short grass with scattered drought – resistant trees.

Human activities depend on climatic characteristics, natural vegetation and types of animals found among other things. For listens, the growing of tea crop is common in mountainous areas, with warm temperatures and heavy rainfall throughout the year, while rearing of sheep for wool production take place in cool temperate regions. A region with relief, climate, vegetation and types of animals, which by their characteristics differ from other regions, is referred to as a *natural region.*

What is Natural Region?
Natural region is a region which possesses a uniformity of relief, climate, natural vegetation, types of animals as well as human activities.

Classification or Division of Natural Regions
The Earth can be divided into the following natural regions:

(a) Equatorial region.

(b) Monsoon region.

(c) Warm temperate margin (Mediterranean) region.

(d) Tropical (savannah) region.

(e) Hot desert region.

(f) Warm temperate Eastern margin (china type) region.

(g) Warm temperate interior region.

(h) Cool temperate western cost margin (British type).

(i) Cool temperate eastern margin (Laurentian type).

(j) Cold temperate continental region.

(k) Tundra and polar region.

(l) Mountain region.

NB: Geographical characteristics of natural region include climate conditions, natural vegetation, types of animals and human activities carried out.

Equatorial Region:

☑ This region is very hot and wet throughout the year.

☑ Have thick forest called *Selves*. The forest dominates tall trees which are always evergreen.

☑ The common trees are mahogany, ebony, rose wood, iron wood and green heart

☑ The forest also consists of three (3) layers, namely;

  (a) Top layer – with very tall tree of about 45 meters high or more

  (b) Middle layer – have tree ferns and lianas which are between 30 to 45 meters high.

☑ Bottom layer – Have herbaceous plants and saprophytes which are less than 30 meters high.

☑ The forest also forms a continuous cover of tree crowns on pot which is known as *canopy*

☑ Animals found in Equatorial region consists of;

  a) Tree dwellers like gorillas, chimpanzees and monkeys

  b) River dwellers such ass hippopotamuses and crocodiles

  c) Open space dwellers such as lions, hyenas zebra, tigers and elephants

  d) There are also birds and insects of various kinds.

☑ The major occupation of the people living in the region is agriculture, where crops like maize, yams, bananas, rubber cocoa and oil palms are grown. Other human activities include Lumbering, fishing as well as industrial work.

Tropical or Savannah Region

It is bordered by both the equatorial regions and the hot deserts. On the parts near the equatorial side there are trees with tall grass, but towards the desert margins, there are short and poor grass accompanied by scattered thorn bushes. These grasslands have different names according to the area where are found. These names are:

* Savannah (Africa and Australia)
* Compos (Brazil)
* Llanos (Venezuela).

Savannah grasslands are the most extensive. Animal found in this natural region are grouped into two categories as follows:

* Fresh – eating animals like lions, hyenas and leopard
* Grass – and leaf– eating animals such as zebra, antelopes, giraffes, elephants, buffaloes, rhinos and hippopotamuses.

The major occupations of the people living in this area are:

* Agriculture, where crops like maize, sugarcane, coffee, bananas, cotton, sisal, millet, beans, tobacco, rice and ground nuts are grown. Kept animals are like cattle goats, sheep and donkeys.
* Fishing, especially on rivers, lakes, oceans and seas
* Other activities include mining, tourism, and manufacturing industries.

Monsoon Region

Natural vegetation in monsoon areas varies due to the variation of rainfall. It consists of forest with trees like cedar, leak, ironwood, sandalwood, and mangrove trees growing along the coast.

Animals are found in small number because their habitats have been reduced due to human population pressure that caused for the increase in need of more land for establishing settlements. Examples of animals found in this region are elephants, tigers and hyenas.

Human Activities in this natural region are; crop cultivations of rice, maize, millet, sorghum and cotton. Livestock kept in this region are cows, goats, sheep, buffaloes and poultry. Other human activities taking place in this region are; fishing, haunting, tourism and manufacturing industries.

Hot Deserts Region

Vegetation found in hot desert region consists of trees which can resist dry condition. Such trees have the following characteristics:

- Have long taproots so as to tap underground water
- Some have few or no leaves so as to reduce loss of water by transpiration
- Others have tough, waxy or needle shaped leaves to minimize transpiration dormant for years but germinate as then get rainfall.
- Many plants produce seeds which lie dormant for years but germinate as they get rainfall.

Good examples of plants which are common in desert region are; cacti and thorny bushes.

The major occupations of the people in desert areas are crop cultivation and animal keeping. The crops grown are date-palm, millet, rice, sugar cane, cotton, tobacco, vines, tomatoes, fruits and vegetables. These crops are mainly grown in oases and along valleys. Animals kept in the region include goat, sheep, donkeys and camels, especially under nomadic herding.

Mediterranean Region

Most of the natural vegetation in this region was cleared for settlement and other socio-economic activities. The vegetation was originally forest consisting of trees like oak, eucalyptus, jar rah and karri. Such trees produce soft wood for paper and furniture making.

Human Activities taking place in this region are:

- Agriculture; where cereals crops and fruits are grown. Cereal crops include wheat, barley, rice and maize while fruits like oranges, lemons, peaches, apricots, plums, pears, grapes, limes, olives and cherries are grown and produced.

- Manufacturing industries, especially fruit canning, wine making, food processing and flour milling are practiced.

Warm Temperate Eastern Margin (China Type) Region

The natural vegetation in this region consists of coniferous forests on highland and deciduous forest in lowlands. Trees which are common include bamboos, oak, camellias, palms, flowering shrubs and camphor.

Human activities taking place include crop cultivation, animal keeping, and lumbering as well as manufacturing industries. Major crop grown are paddy, maize, cotton, tobacco and sugar cane. Dairy cattle are also kept for the production of milk, butter and cheese.

Warm Temperate Interior Region

The natural vegetation found in this region is mainly grass. These grasslands have specific names depending on where they are found like identified below:

- Veldt (South Africa)
- Pampas (Argentina)
- Downs (Australia)

Major occupations of people are cattle rearing, growing of crops and industrial activities. Animas kept are cattle for beef and dairy, sheep for wool. Farming involve the production of wheat, maize and fruits leading to agricultural-based industries such as meat canning, fruit canning as well as manufacturing of starch.

Cool Temperate West Coast Margin

Natural vegetation found in the region is favored by the climatic condition. It consists of evergreen coniferous forests which predominate in the mountain areas and broad-leafed deciduous trees in other areas. Major activities are:

- Agriculture – that involves arable farming, horticulture, animal farming and mixed farming. Crop grown include wheat, barley, oats and apples.

- Other active – There is also mining where minerals like coal and iron are available especially in north-west Europe.

Cool Temperate Eastern Margin (Laurentian Type)

The vegetation is this region consists mainly of coniferous and deciduous forests. Trees like oak and beech are common. Major occupations of the people are farming and manufacturing. Crops like wheat, maize, millet and soya beans are grown.

Cold Temperate Continental Region

Natural vegetation found in this region is mainly coniferous forests. Due to cold temperatures, trees are slow growing and evergreen. Human activities taking place include lumbering, agriculture and manufacturing industries.

Crop grown include wheat and other temperate cereals, such as barley and oats. There also mixed farming. Many industries deal with the processing of agricultural crop and timber. Wood is mainly for making pulp for paper.

Tundra and Polar Regions

These regions have very low temperatures and therefore, they have scanty vegetation. The main activities carried out by Eskimos of North America and the Lapps of Eurasia are hunting and fishing. Animals found include caribou, reindeers and bears. Also people do fishing for whales, walrus and seals. People in this area fish and fat are their main food. There is no agriculture of any type.

Mountain Regions

There are various natural vegetation zones in mountain region due to variation of altitudes. The vegetation zones on African mountains are:

- ☑ Savannah with dry bush, savannah grass land and woodlands.
- ☑ Rainforests both tropical evergreens and temperate forests
- ☑ Bamboo forest
- ☑ Heath and moorland where grass, shrubs and flowers are becoming more and sparser at upper levels.

The major occupations of the people in this region are lumbering, agriculture, and pastoralism. As the mountains receive heavy rainfall, waterfalls on the lower slopes are utilized to generate hydroelectric power, leading to industrial development.

Relationship between Human Activities and Climate

Human activities are activities that man engages in, so as to earn a living. The best human activities are crop cultivation, livestock rearing, fishing, lumbering, hunting and gathering.

Climate has a direct relationship with human activities. These human activities according to the climatic types are as distributed as it is going to be discussed.

(1) Equatorial Climate

This is warm and rainy zone with dense forests. In this climate, human activities carried out are:

a. Hutting and food collection. This done by the more primitive people.

b. Shuffling cultivation that done by more advanced dwellers.

177

c. Crops are sometimes grown on plantation. For example rubber (in Malaysia Liberia and Indonesia), Oil palm (in Malaysia Nigeria and D.R.C) and sugar cane (in Cuba).

d. Small peasant holdings (e.g. cocoa in Ghana and Ivory Coast).

e. Timber industries have been developed due to the presence of mahogany, ebony and green heart trees.

f. Development become difficult in this region because of diseases and pests and poor soil which lose humus easily after the forest cover is cleared.

(2) Tropical Continental Climate

This region characterized by natural vegetation which consists of tall grass with scattered trees. The region is inhabited by livestock-keeping tribes such as Maasai who are nomadic and flans at West Africa.

Crops grown are millet, maize, bananas, ground nuts and beans which are used for food while cash crops are cotton, tobacco, sugar cane and sisal. The main factors that hinder agriculture development are unreliable rainfall, diseases and pests, loss of soil fertility and poor communication.

(3) Tropical Marine Climate

The region receives rainfall almost every month with heavier falls in the hot season because of onshore trade winds which blow throughout the year. The main human activities are crop cultivation, especially food crop in most parts of the West Indies, East Africa and Queensland in North East Australia. Other crop grown is coffee.

(4) Tropical Desert Climate

Rainfall is scarce and the region is hot. People who live onshore region engage in human activities like:

a) Cultivation along oases where dates, wheat, vegetable and fruits are grown.

b) Normandy herding takes place in Arabia and Sahara deserts. There are larger herds of goats, sheep and camels which are grazed on poor desert vegetation.

c) The shore lands of the river valleys such as Nile, Tigris and Euphrates are intensively cultivated for both food and cash crops.

(5) *Warn Temperate Western Margin Climate*

The region receives low rainfall during the winter. During summer, the region is hot. In this climate, people engage in the following human activities:

a. Cultivation of olive trees that rich in oil

b. Citrus fruit cultivation-through irrigation. The main producers are Chile, Israel etc.

c. Wheat and barley are grown mainly in winter.

d. Tobacco and cotton are also grown in this region

e. Cultivation of grapes, known as viticulture. Grape fruits are used to make wine.

(6) *Warm Temperate Interior Climate*

The region characterized by grass as the natural vegetation. Large herds of beef cattle and wool sheep are reared in these grasslands.

(7) *Warm Temperate Eastern Margin Climate*

The region receives rainfall throughout the year because the trade winds are onshore and the westerlies winds are offshore. This region, favor for continuous crop growing throughout the year.

The people of this region, engages in agriculture. Crop grown are rice (china), cotton, maize and tobacco (South Eastern USA). Maize uses for fattening pigs and cattle. Cattle, and sheep, are also kept in this region.

(8) *Cool Temperate Western Margin Climate*

The region is cool in temperate and wet. The onshore westerlies winds prevent the region from freezing. This region has the following human activities:

a. Farming activities as wheat barley and oats
b. Fruit farming like apple in British Columbia
c. Cattle and sheep farming for wool and meet (New Zealand, Chile etc.)

(9) *Cool Temperate Eastern Margin*

The region is cold in winter and warm in summer. This climate is ideal for the following human activities:

a) Mixed farming with cattle, oats, and wheat (is the major activities in the low lands of North East America)
b) Market gardening
c) Fruit farming for apples is very important in some areas.
d) Crops farming are wheat, maize, millet and soya beans.

(10) Cool Temperate Interior Climate:

The climate has low temperatures. This type is ideal for cultivation of wheat in large farming units. This is very important in Eurasia and America. Mixed farming, usually cattle with wheat and other temperate cereals, take place in Europe and Russia.

(11) Cold Temperate Continental Climate

The region is very cold. The subsoil is frozen for most parts of the year and this prevents most types of agriculture to take place. There hunting done by the cold region dwellers.

(12) Tundra Climate

In this climate, the sub-soil is permanently frozen and there is no possibility of any form of agriculture. However, tree cutting and hunting activities are taking place.

(13) Polar Climate

The region is covered by ice throughout. There is no way of conducting any form of agriculture. There are mining activities taking place in the region.

(14) Mountains Climate

The mountains have a variety of climate starting from the foot to the peak. However, the mountain slopes are very important for crop cultivation. Coffee and flowers are very famous on most mountain slopes of the tropical land. Animal rearing is an important human activity on the mountains. Valleys provide grass and shelter during winter seasons.

Climatic Change

Climate change is a change in the statistical distribution of weather patterns when that change lasts for an extended period of time (i.e. decades to millions of years). In a different way of defining climate change it can be defined as a change in average weather conditions, or in the time variation of weather around longer-term average conditions (i.e., more or fewer extreme weather events).

Climate change is caused by factors such as biotic processes, variations in solar radiation received by Earth, plate tectonics, and volcanic eruptions. Certain human activities have also been identified as significant causes of recent climate change, often referred to as *global warming*. Sometimes climatic can change over a time, especially when its element have been influenced by different factors.

Factors for Climate Changes

The following are some of the factors influencing climate to change:

1. Volcanic eruption; which emit greenhouse gases and dust in the atmosphere.

2. Tectonic of plates; movement of oceanic and continental plates lead to experiencing of new climatic types.

3. Continental drifts; the continents drifted from the origin landmass can be situated to another type climatic condition.

4. Human activities; all human activities undertaken on the earth are directly causing climatic change.

5. Effects to the atmosphere like global warming

Effects of Climatic Change

Effects caused by climatic change may lead to the following impacts:

1. *Occurrence of drought:* This is due to the excessive produced heat and temperature on the earth's land surface from the sun. The depleted ozone layer allow free pass of sun rays leading to the high heating that cause increase of temperature on the land surface, which may influence for the occurrence of drought.

2. *Occurrence of floods:* fostered by the increase of temperature on the earth's surface, in which caused by high heat produced by the sun. Increase of temperature tends to increase the rate of evaporation and ice or snow melts that leading to the occurrence of high precipitation and increase of volume in water bodies.

3. *Desertification:* Occur due to the loss and decline of trees and vegetation cover on the earth's surface, in which it is caused by volcanic eruptions and excessive human activities that leading to the climatic change.

4. *Migration and displacement of species:* is the one that influenced by the impact of the climatic change. Living organism may displace or migrate on the area due to the occurrence of drought and floods that influenced by increase of temperature as the result of global warming on an area.

5. *Eruption of diseases:* diseases like skin cancer, malnutrition, communicable diseases and water bone disease may erupt due to the ozone depletion, poor food supply, air pollution and water pollution and poor sanitation respectively are due to the effect caused by change of climate.

6. *Formation of acidic rain:* volcanic eruptions and human activities like mining activities, agricultural activities, and industrial activities undertaken on the earth are directly causing for the formation of acidic rain due the supply of chemical and acidic gases to the atmosphere.

6. *Ozone layer depletion:* Volcanic eruption, use of refrigerator, sprays among others which emit greenhouse gases and dust in the atmosphere lead to the impact or depletion to the ozonosphere.

Solutions to Climatic Problems
There are natural and human-made causes of climatic changes and the change bring about problems of climate.

The following are possible solution to climatic problems:

(1) *Provision of Environmental Education.* There should be provided education to the people so as to know the advantages of maintenance and conserving the environment, so as to restore better climate hence preventing occurrence of climate problems.

(2) *Avoidance of Bad menthols of farming:* Bad methods of farming are prevalent in developing countries including Tanzania. Such methods are like shifting cultivation, over use of inorganic fertilizers, irregular farming along slopes and others. Such farming brings about desertification which in turn brings climatic problems. If people avoid such methods then climatic problems will, at least, be reduced

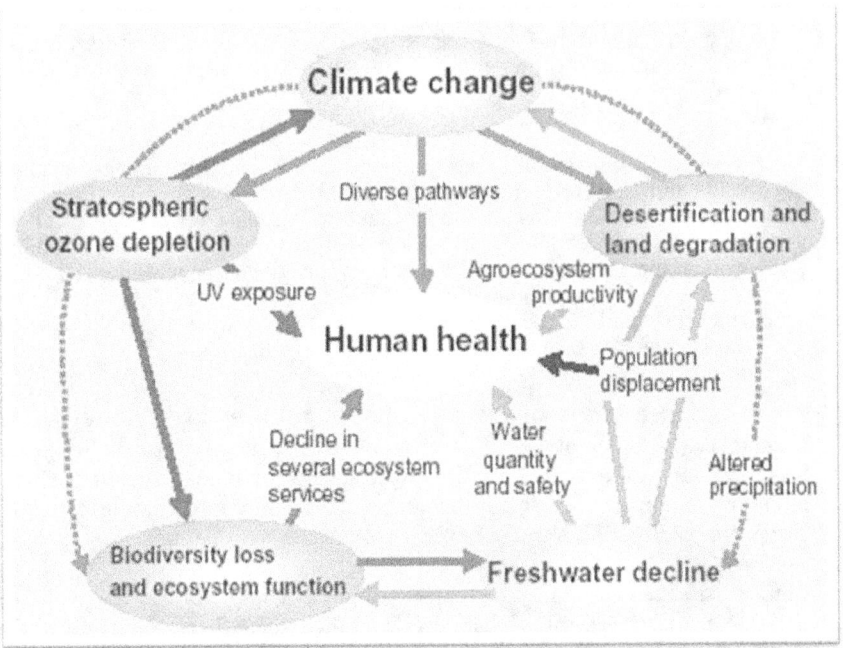

Fig.11.1: Outcome and effects of climatic change

(3) *Afforestation:* This is the common technique used to plant trees after being harvested. This reduces desertification and then minimizes the emanation of climatic problems

(4) *Formulation of laws and Rules:* Countries should enact laws and rules from national level to local level so as to guard the environment and in so doing reduce climatic problems

(5) *Reduction of carbon dioxide from industries:* Measures to reduce carbon dioxide added to the atmosphere is through minimizing industrial carbon dioxide output and maintaining plants which consume carbon dioxide to safeguard the ozone layer (O_3) is also a solution to climatic problems.

(6) *Application of good methods of farming:* People or nations that greatly rely on crop farming and animal farming should do so by employing

environmental friendly techniques like proper density farming as per the capacity of the environment, Use organic manure or fertilizers, proper irrigation procedures and others so as to avoid climatic problems.

(7) Application of appropriate technology: For developed countries, this is a habit but in developing countries, people are still using inappropriate technology. Measures should be taken to emphasize the application of appropriate technology so as to: Provide jobs for people, Produce goods for local markets, Replace imported goods with local goods which are of the same quality, Use local resource, labor and raw materials and finances, Provide communities with serves like health, water, housing and education.

In depth study of Climate Change on the Earth Planet

Climate is made up of elements that are the same as those of weather. Climatic change is directly or indirectly influenced by human activities which alter the composition of the global-atmosphere and which may lead to the climate variability that observed over reasonable time of periods.

Climatic change can be into extreme warming or cooling of the atmosphere. Extreme warming at the global level is called *'global warming'*. Climatic change it is not an overnight process, but it involves gradual process. If climatic change might involve sudden change, it can cause for destruction since the life system and economies have no sufficient time to adopt the change.

Factors Influencing Distribution of Climate

The followings are the factors that affect the climate: Altitude, Aspect, Latitudes, Distance from the sea, Ocean currents, Prevailing winds, Alignment of the coastline among others:

Latitude

- Latitude affluences temperature on the surface of the earth.
- Areas nearer to the equator experience higher rainfall and temperature than those further away.
- Seasonal variation of Rainfall is partly influenced by latitude.
- The influence of latitude also extends to pressure systems of the world and behavior of winds as well.
- Also latitude influence the intensity of sunshine

Altitude

@ This factor influence temperature and atmospheres pressure of a region.

184

@ Low-altitude region are warmer and experience high atmospheres pressure while High altitude are cooler and have low atmospheric pressure.

@ Where prevailing winds are moist more rainfall is experienced at high altitudes than at low altitudes

Distance from the Sea or Ocean

♯ This factor is also referred to as the effect of nearer to the sea or continental

♯ The influence of the sea is both on temperature and rainfall of a region.

♯ With regard to rainfall onshore winds bring rainfall to the land and coastal areas are the first to benefit from them. This causes coastal regions to be very wet

Aspect

§ Aspect refers to the direction in which a slope faces.

§ Windward slopes of highlands receive much higher rainfall than the leeward slopes.

Ocean Currents

⤙ Ocean current flowing along the coast tend to modify the climate of the coastal regions

⤙ Where onshore winds blow over a cold ocean current, they are cooled from below and the moisture they are carrying is condensed and dropped over the sea as rain.

⤙ Cold currents have desert type of climate. This results in an insular climate along the coast.

Prevailing Winds

🖋 Winds are a medium of transfer of heat and moisture over the land.

🖋 If wind is blowing from a warm region it has a warming effect aver the region it is blowing across. Find if the wind originates from a cold region, it will also be cold and will cool the land over which it is blowing.

Alignment of the Coastline

◎ This factor is also referred to as configuration of the coastline, is positioned in relation to prevailing onshore winds.

◎ Where the onshore winds blow transversely to the shore, they cause heavy rainfall along the coast.

Human Activities

Human activities such as development of settlements, clearing of forest, draining and cultivating swampy areas, emission of chlorofluorocarbons and other gases from factories and motor vehicles, construction of dams and creation of man-made lakes have a considerable influence on climate distribution, especially on local areas.

185

Causes of Global Climatic Change

Causes of global climatic change involve natural and human causes:

1. Natural causes:

(i). The impacts of asteroids and cosmic radiation from exploding stars called *supernovas*.

(ii). Massive volcanic eruption that emit greenhouse gases and lot of dusts deposited to the atmosphere.

(iii). Changes in solar energy associated with 11-years sunspots cycles or 22-yeasrs solar magnetic cycles might play the role.

(iv). Tectonics and oceans spreading which change the location of the land masses through drifting.

2. Human causes:

They are influenced by human activities (anthropogenic factors) such as: development of settlement, agriculture, clearing of forest, draining and cultivating swamp areas, emission of chlorofluorocarbons and other gases from factories and motor vehicles. Therefore, when people fail to take precaution about their activities, the global climate will eventually change its characteristics.

Question: Suggest ways to reduce or control the effects of climatic change at local and international level.

Global Warming and Greenhouse

Greenhouse refers to the situation in which the atmosphere traps and retains heat energy from the sun in the lower levels leading to the rise in temperature. The atmosphere traps the heat with greenhouse gases that hang in it such as carbon dioxide added to the atmosphere through burning of fossil fuels (methane (CH_4) released from ruminant animals, decomposing wet rice paddies, coal mines, landfills and pipe leaks; Chlorofluorocarbons, released from refrigerators and insecticides, nitrous oxide (N_2O) from burning organic materials and soil denitrification, perfluorocarbons and sulphur hexafluoride.

Green gases tend to trap heat from the sun and keep it in the lower levels since the energy radiated from the surface has long wavelength, hence cannot penetrate through the gases and get lost into the space. USA is the leading country in producing carbon dioxide that contribute to the global warming about 63.6%; methane about 19%, CFCs about 11% and Nitrous oxide about 6%; the burning of fossil fuels contributes to about 49%, industrial processes contribute to about 24%, deforestation contributes to about 14% and agriculture about 13%.

Effects of Greenhouse and Global Warming

The global warming that caused by greenhouse effects have led to the following effects:

1. The rise of temperature has led to the melting of ice in various parts of the world. E.g. Melting of ice cap on mountains like Kilimanjaro and melting of ice sheets in Antarctic has increased.

2. The melting of ice has led to the increase of water in the sea, hence the rise of sea levels lead to the occurrence of floods at some coastal areas.

3. Global warming has led to the occurrences of strong storms that kills people and destroy property in different parts of the world.

4. Cold areas have become warm, such that tropical crops are grown successfully.

5. Extinction of some animal and plant species due to failure to adapt to the abrupt rise in temperature.

6. Prevalence of drought conditions in various parts of the world, affecting food production.

7. Occurrence of precipitation in other areas, which used to be dry due to the change in hydrological cycle.

8. Flood and droughts have led to massive migration of animals and human beings.

9. Decline of production, hence increase of poverty and prevalence of famine (a case study in Africa)

Measures to Solve the Effects of Global Warming and Greenhouse Effect:

1. Discouraging the use and burning materials that release harmful greenhouse gases, such as fossil fuels and coals.

2. Promotion in the use of alternative energy sources which are environmental friendly e.g. geothermal power, solar energy and wind energy.

3. Encouraging people use public transit and not private cars or to walk more than using car so as to reduce an emission of greenhouse gases.

4. Modification of the combustion system in the machine in order to attain efficient fuel burning and curb massive release of greenhouse gases, particularly carbon dioxide.

5. Formulation and implementation of international policies and cooperation of nations in the fight to reduce air pollution that leads to the additional of greenhouse gases in the atmosphere.

6. Large scale agriculture in rice cultivation should be improved so as to cut off the release of methane gas.

7. There should be a recycling of the wastes rather than burning or dumping on the earth's land surface.

Activity: Discuss for the causes of desertification, effects of desertification and measures to be checked in order to curb effects caused by desertification.

GLOSSARY

Absolute Humidity: it is the vapor concentration or vapor density

Adiabatic lapse rate: the lapse rate which occurs when the temperature changes without addition or substitution of energy.

Aerosols: these are particulate matters.

Air mass: the large body or volume of air with uniform characteristics of temperature and humidity moving or covering a large area and moving along a considerable long distance.

Albedo: the ratio between incoming radiation and the amount reflected back into space expressed in percentage.

Altitude: the height of the ground measured from the mean sea level.

Anemometer: a tool measuring velocity or speed of wind.

Angle of incidence: The angle which rays from the sun strikes the earth's surface.

Anticyclones: Are reverse of depression whereby air circulates away from the centre in a clockwise motion in the northern hemisphere and anti-clockwise in the southern hemisphere.

Aspect: the direction of to which a slope of the land masses faces the sun.

Atmosphere: the thin layer of gases, particulate matter and biotic matter held to the earth by gravitational attraction.

Atmospheric instability: the condition where the earth's atmosphere is generally unstable due to weather being high in degree of variability through distance and time.

Atmospheric stability: the condition which the air in the atmosphere tends to rise or resist depending on weather condition surrounding areas.

Barometer: a tool that measures air pressure.

Bora: an extremely cold and dry wind north westerly which blows along the shore of the Adriatic Sea.

Campbell stock sunshine recorder: an instrument used for measuring and recording the duration of sunshine.

Capacity humidity: the ratio of mass of water vapor to that of the air coming it.

Climate: it is the average of weather conditions of an area which are observed, recorded and analyzed over a considerable long period of time (usually 30 years or over).

Climatic change: the change in the statistical distribution of weather patterns when that change lasts for an extended period of time.

Climatology: it is the study of physical atmospheric condition particularly weather and climate together.

Cloud cover: it is the mixture of water droplets and ice produced by condensation in the atmosphere.

Condensation: the process through which atmospheric water vapor is converted into liquid as a result of cooling.

Conduction: it is the movement of heat energy from one molecule to another without changes in their relative position.

Convergence zones: are the regions where two air mass meet.

Coriolis forces: are forces created by the rotation of the earth and sometimes they are known as Ferrelis Law of Deflection.

Cyclones: are centre of low pressure surrounded by closed isobars having increased pressure outward.

Divergence zones: are the areas where two air masses move away from one another.

Doldrums: are winds formed and found along or near equator which are known as equatorial wind system.

Drizzle: the fall of numerous uniform minutes' droplets of water having diameter of less than 0.5mm.

Earth's net radiation: the balance between incoming and outgoing energy at top of the atmosphere.

Environmental lapse rate: the situation whereby temperature decreases by increase of altitude.

Evaporation: the process in which liquid water turns into water vapor and rise up.

Evaporimeter: a tool that measures the rate and amount of evaporation.

Exosphere: the last layer which reaches beyond 960km from the earth's surface.

Fog: a thin cloud consisting of microscopically small water droplets which are kept in suspension in the air near the surface and reduces the horizontal visibility to greater than 1km.

Front: a line or zone where two contrasting air masses converge or meet.

Gaseous matter: are permanent gases and fixed in volume, including nitrogen, oxygen, carbon dioxide, ozone and argon.

Global warming: a gradual increase in world temperature caused by polluting gases such as carbon dioxide which are collecting in the air around the earth and prevent heat escaping into space.

Greenhouse: it is the situation in which the atmosphere traps and retains heat energy from the sun in the lower levels leading to the rise in temperature.

Hail: is the one of the components in precipitation which consists of large pallets of ice that are known as hailstone having diameter of 50mm.

Harmattan: the warm and dry wind blowing from east-west across Sahara desert.

Heat: the amount of energy in a body.

Heat budget: the balance between the amount of solar radiation received by the earth's surface and its atmosphere and the amount of heat lost from the earth by outgoing terrestrial long wave radiation from the earth's surface and lost heat from the atmosphere.

Horse latitude winds: these are winds develops in area where the trade winds and westerly winds diverge.

Humidity: the amount of water vapor or moisture in the atmosphere.

Hurricanes: the extensive tropical cyclones surrounded by close isobars.

Hydrological cycle: the endless or continuous process interchanges of water between the atmosphere, the land and water bodies.

Hygrometer: an instrument for measuring water vapour content of air or relative humidity of the air.

Insolation: the amount of solar energy received at the earth's surface.

Isobars: Are lines drawn on the map showing pressure.

Isobaths: Are lines drawn on the map showing water depth.

Isohels: Are lines drawn on the map showing sunshine.

Isohyets: Are lines drawn on the map showing rainfall.

Isotherms: Are lines drawn on the map showing temperature.

Jetstream: are the strongest belt of winds formed near the tropopause and they blow from west to east.

Lapse rate: the situation whereby temperature decrease with the increase in altitude or increase with decrease of altitude.

Line-squall: is the word meaning to a sudden strong winds or short storms.

Long wave radiation: the energy radiating from the earth as infrared radiation at low energy to space.

Mesosphere: the third layer extending to about 80 – 90km separated from the stratosphere by the layer (Ozone) of discontinuity called stratopause.

Meteorology: the scientific study dealing with the atmosphere and its phenomena, including weather and climate.

Mistral: Is the cold wind which commonly blows in Spain and France from north-west to south-west direction.

Monsoon: is an Arabic word meaning season. Therefore, monsoon wind is the season wind.

Natural region: a region which possesses a uniformity of relief, climate, natural vegetation, types of animals as well as human activities.

Ozonosphere: the lower region of stratosphere containing relatively concentration of ozone.

Precipitation: a falling down of water, moisture or frozen water from the atmosphere towards the earth's surface.

Pressure (atmospheric pressure): the force applied at a point in the earth's surface due to the weight of air above that point.

Radiation: the process by which heat energy is emitted from a body.

Rainfall: one of the precipitation whereby water droplets falls from high in the atmosphere into the earth's surface.

Rain gauge: an instrument that measures the amount of rain that has fallen over a specific time period.

Reflection: the ability of an object to reflect waves without altering either the object or the waves

Relative humidity: the ratio of the amount of water vapour actually presented in the air having definite volume and temperature.

Sirocco: is a warm, dry and dusty winds blow in northern direction from Sahara desert.

Sleet: one of precipitation form, which involves mixture of snow and rain at the same time.

Snow: one of precipitation form, formed when water vapour condenses at a temperature below freezing point passing directly from the gaseous to sold state and forming minute speckles of ice.

Stevenson's screen: the white wooden box which is mounted on four legs, used to house the hygrometer and thermometer for measuring humidity and temperature respectively.

Stratosphere: the second layer which extends to about 50km from the earth's surface. It is also known as ozonosphere.

Sublimation: the process in which water vapor changes directly into sold state without passing through liquid state.

Sunshine: the sun's rays that reach the surface of the earth.

Temperate cyclones: are atmospheric disturbances having low pressure in the centre and increasing pressure outward.

Temperature: the degree of hotness or coldness of an object or a place.

Temperature inversion: an increase in temperature with height or to the layer (inversion layer) within which such an increase occurs.

Thermometer: an instrument that used for measuring temperature.

Thermosphere: this is the fourth layer in the atmosphere which is separated from mesosphere by ozone of discontinuity known as mesospause.

Thunderstorms: are local storms characterized by cloud thunder and lightning.

Tornadoes: are dark funnel shaped storms which are smallest but most violet disastrous of all storms.

Transmission: the process whereby a wave passes completely through a medium as when light waves are transmitted.

Tropical cyclones: are cyclones normally developed in the region lying between the tropics of Capricorn and cancer.

Troposphere: the first lowest bottom layer in the atmosphere.

Water spouts: are storms that characterized by rapid whirling water drops sent out with great force caused by intense pressure system that is similar to a tornado which develops over the sea.

Water vapour: the suspended liquid particles in the atmosphere.

Weather: the atmospheric condition of a place which occurs at a particular short period of time.

Weather forecasting: the prediction of weather conditions of an area at a given time.

Weather station: a place where observation, measuring and recording of weather elements takes place.

Wind: is the movement of air from high pressure to low pressure.

Wind vane: an instrument uses for measuring direction of wind blow.

REFERENCES

Barry, R. and Chorley. (1972). *Atmosphere, Weather and Climate.* Methuen, London.

Botikin, D.B. and Keller, E. (1982). *Environmental Studies: The Earth as a living planet.* Mellir Publishing Company, Columbus.

Buckle, C. (1978). *Landforms in Africa:* Longman, London.

Briggs, K. (1985). *Physical Geography: Process and System:* London, Holder and Stoughton.

Bunnet, R. B. (2003). *Physical Geography in Diagrams for Africa:* England, Longman 26th Edition.

Bunnet, R. B. (2003). *General Geography in Diagrams:* New edition (46th impression), Singapore.

Clark, A. N. (1985). *Dictionary of Geography:* London, Longman.

Collin and Longman. (1980). *Fariran, A and Ojo, O: man's Physical Environment:* H.E.B, London.

Critchfield, H. J., (1974). *General Climatology, 3rd Edition.* Prentice Hall, Inc. Egglewood Cliffs, New Jersey.

Henderson-Sellers, A. and Robinson, P., (1986). *Contemporary climatology. Longman.* Essex

manJfose, F. J. (1978). *A Dictionary of the Natural Environment:* London, Edward Anold.

McKnight, T.L., (1986), *Physical Geography: A Landscape Appreciation, 5th Edition.*

Monkhouse, F. J. (2004). *Principles of Physical Geography:* 90 Totten ham Court Road, London Wip 9HE.

Pearcy, W. G, Schoener, A., (1987). *"Changes in the marine biota coincident with the 1982-83 El Nino in the north eastern Subarctic Pacific Ocean"* Journal of Geography Research 92(13): 14417-14428.

The Great Soviet Encyclopedia, (1979). *Weather and Climatology.*